Math in Focus®

FOCUS®

Singapore Math®
by Marshall Cavendish

Student Edition

Program Consultant and Author
Dr. Fong Ho Kheong

Authors
Chelvi Ramakrishnan
Michelle Choo

U.S. Distributor

mc **Marshall Cavendish**
Education

Houghton Mifflin Harcourt.
The Learning Company™

Grade
2A

Contents

2 Addition Within 1,000

Hands-on Activity

25 + 6

Chapter

Using Bar Models: Addition and Subtraction

5 Length

▶ Hands-on Activity

© 2020 Marshall Cavendish Education Pte Ltd

Mass

Manipulative List

10–sided die

Base 10 blocks

Base 10 unit

Base 10 rod

Base 10 hundred-square

Base 10 thousand-cube

Connecting cubes

Place value strips

Transparent counters

Preface

Welcome!

Math in Focus® is a program that puts **you** at the center of an exciting learning experience! This experience is all about helping you to really understand math and become a strong and confident problem solver!

What is in your book?

Each chapter in this book begins with a real-world example of the math topic you are about to learn.

In each chapter, you will see these features:

THINK provides a problem for the whole section, to get you thinking. If you cannot answer the problem right away, you can come back to it a few times as you work through the section.

ENGAGE contains tasks that link what you already know with what you will be learning next. You can explore and discuss the tasks with your classmates.

LEARN introduces you to new math concepts using examples and activities, where you can use objects to help you learn.

Hands-on Activity gives you the chance to work closely with your classmates, using objects or drawing pictures, to help you learn math.

TRY gives you the chance to practice what you are learning, with support.

INDEPENDENT PRACTICE allows you to work on different kinds of problems, and to use what you have learned to solve these problems on your own.

Additional features include:

RECALL PRIOR KNOWLEDGE	 Math Talk	MATH SHARING	GAME
Helps you recall related concepts you learned before, accompanied by practice questions	Invites you to talk about your thinking and communicate your ideas to your classmates and teachers	Encourages you to create strategies, discover methods, and share them with your classmates and teachers using mathematical language	Helps you to really master the concepts you learned, through fun partner games
LET'S EXPLORE	MATH JOURNAL	PUT ON YOUR THINKING CAP!	CHAPTER WRAP-UP
Extends your learning through investigation	Allows you to reflect on your learning when you write down your thoughts about the concepts learned	Challenges you to apply the concepts to solve problems in different ways	Summarizes your learning in a flow chart and helps you to make connections within the chapter
CHAPTER REVIEW	Assessment Prep	PERFORMANCE TASK	STEAM
Provides you with a lot of practice in the concepts learned	Prepares you for state tests with assessment-type problems	Assesses your learning through problems that allow you to demonstrate your understanding and knowledge	Promotes collaboration with your classmates through interesting projects that allow you to use math in creative ways

Let's begin your exciting learning journey with us! Are you ready?

Numbers to 1,000

How do we read the numbers?

Which number is the least? Which number is the greatest?

How can you use a place-value chart to compare three numbers?

Name: _____ Date: _____

Counting on

Count on by tens and ones.

10, …, 20, …, 30, …, 40, …, 50, …, 60, …, 70, …, 80, …, 90, …, 100, …, 110, 111, 112, 113

There are 113 sticks.

▶ **Quick Check**

Count on by tens and ones.
Fill in each blank.

1

10, …, 20, …, 30, …, 40, …, 50, …, 60, …, 70, …, 80, …,

90, …, _____, …, _____, 111, 112, 113, 114, 115, 116,

117, _____, _____

There are _____ .

Reading and writing numbers

Number: 107   Word: one hundred seven

▶ **Quick Check**

Fill in each blank with the correct number.

2 one hundred five   _____

3 one hundred eighteen   _____

Write each number in words.

4 112 _____

5 120 _____

Reading place-value charts

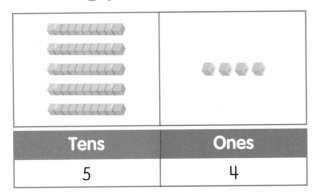

Tens	Ones
5	4

54 = 5 tens 4 ones
54 = 50 + 4

▶ **Quick Check**

Fill in each blank.

6 40 and _____ make 48.

7 63 is _____ and 3.

8 _____ + 9 = 79

Comparing numbers

	Tens	Ones
50	5	0
34	3	4

Compare the tens.
5 tens are greater than 3 tens.

So, 50 is greater than 34.
50 > 34

We can also say that 34 is less than 50.
34 < 50

▶ **Quick Check**

Fill in each blank with TRUE or FALSE.

9 29 is greater than 43.   _____

10 69 < 96   _____

Ordering numbers

	Tens	Ones
85	8	5
82	8	2
95	9	5

STEP 1 Compare the tens.
9 tens are greater than 8 tens.
So, 95 is the greatest.

STEP 2 The tens in the other two numbers are the same.
So, compare the ones.
2 ones are less than 5 ones.
So, 82 is the least.

From least to greatest, the numbers are:

82   85   95
least   greatest

▶ **Quick Check**

**Compare and order the numbers from greatest to least.
Fill in each blank.**

74   67   77

⑪ The greatest number is _____.

⑫ The least number is _____.

⑬ _____ _____ _____
        greatest   least

Making number patterns

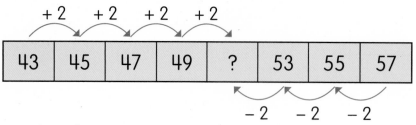

2 more than 49 is 51.
2 less than 53 is 51.

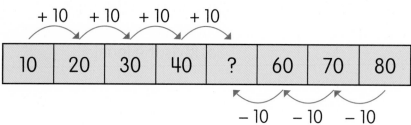

10 more than 40 is 50.
10 less than 60 is 50.

▶ **Quick Check**

The numbers are arranged in a pattern.
Find each missing number.

14

60   58   56   54

15

72   74   76   78   84

16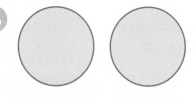

70   80   90   100

Counting to 1,000

Learning Objectives:
- Use base-ten blocks to count, read, and write numbers to 1,000.
- Count on by 1s, 10s, and 100s to 1,000.

New Vocabulary
thousand
hundreds

THINK

Look at the numbers.
Count and fill in each missing number in order.

_____, _____, 410, 411, _____, _____,

_____, 415

ENGAGE

1. Count on by ones from 100 to find the next three numbers.

2. Count on by tens from 100 to find the next three numbers.

3. Count on by hundreds from 100 to find the next three numbers.

LEARN Count to 1,000

1. Put 10 🟦 together to make ▬▬▬▬▬.

10
one ten

10, 20, 30, 40, 50,
60, 70, 80, 90, **100**

Put 10 ▬▬▬▬▬ together to make ▦.

100
one hundred

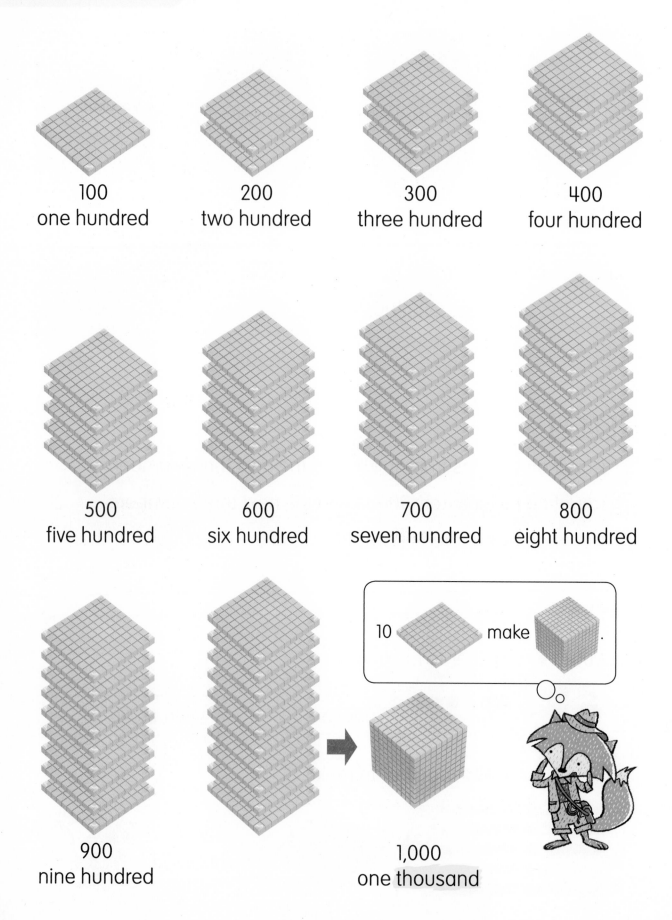

100
one hundred

200
two hundred

300
three hundred

400
four hundred

500
five hundred

600
six hundred

700
seven hundred

800
eight hundred

900
nine hundred

1,000
one thousand

10   make   .

2

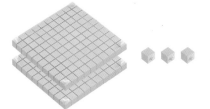

203
two hundred three

100, …, 200, 201, 202, **203**

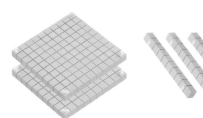

230
two hundred thirty

100, …, 200, …, 210, …, 220, …, **230**

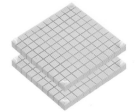

234
two hundred thirty-four

100, …, 200, …, 210, …, 220, …, 230, 231, 232, 233, **234**

3 Count on by ones.

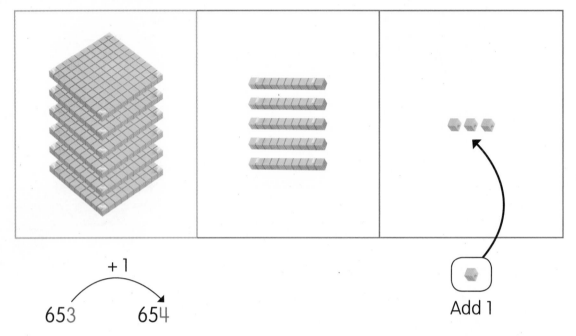

+1

653 → 654

Add 1

4 Count on by tens.

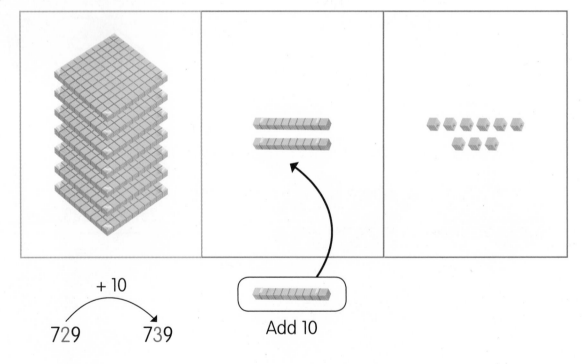

+10

729 → 739

Add 10

5 Count on by hundreds.

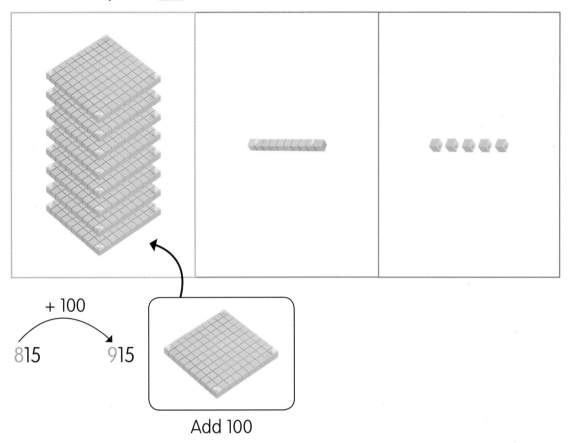

+ 100

815 → 915

Add 100

Hands-on Activity Showing and writing numbers

Work in pairs.

① Think of a 3-digit number and tell it to your partner.

② Ask your partner to use to show the number.

③ Check your partner's answer.

④ Trade places.

Repeat ① to ③ three times.

TRY Practice counting to 1,000

Count on.
Fill in each blank.

1

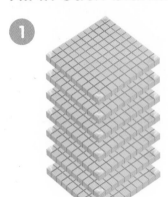

100, …, 200, …, 300, …, 400, …, _____, …,

_____, …, _____, …, 710, …, _____,

721, _____, _____, _____, _____

There are _____ 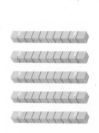.

Find each missing number.

2

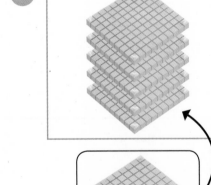

+ 100   + 100

557 _____   _____   _____

Name: _____ Date: _____

INDEPENDENT PRACTICE

Count.
Fill in each blank.

_____

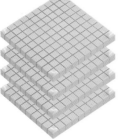

_____

_____

Count on by ones, tens, or hundreds.
Find each missing number.

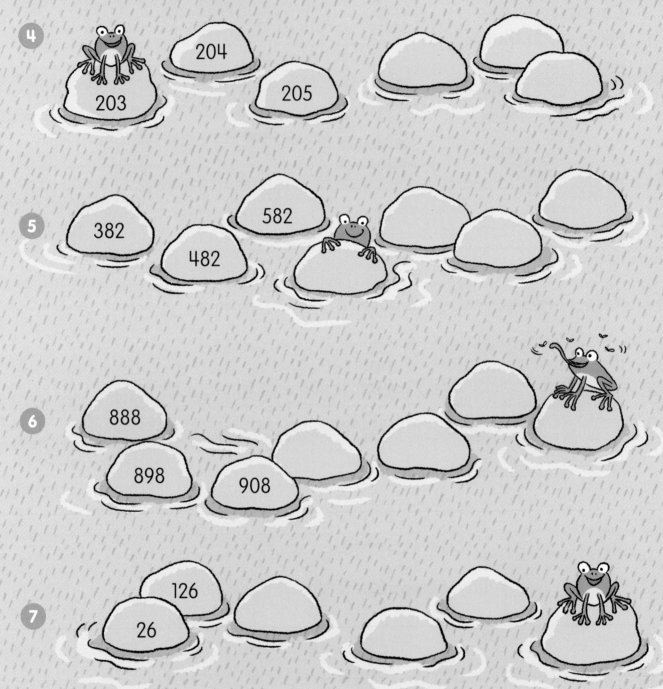

4 203 204 205

5 382 482 582

6 888 898 908

7 26 126

Name: _____ Date: _____

Place Value

Learning Objectives:
- Use a place-value chart to read, write, and represent numbers to 1,000.
- Read and write numbers to 1,000 in expanded form, standard form, and word form.

New Vocabulary
expanded form
standard form
word form

THINK

How many 3-digit numbers can you make with these three cards?

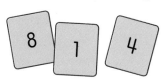

Does the least number end with 1?
Why?

What is the value of the digits in the numbers you make?
What is the value of the digit 1 in the least number?

ENGAGE

1. Use  and a place-value chart to show these numbers.

   a 5 **b** 50 **c** 500

   Show 50 on the place-value chart in another way.

2. What are the missing numbers?

   734 = 7 hundreds 2 tens _____ ones

   = 7 hundreds _____ ones

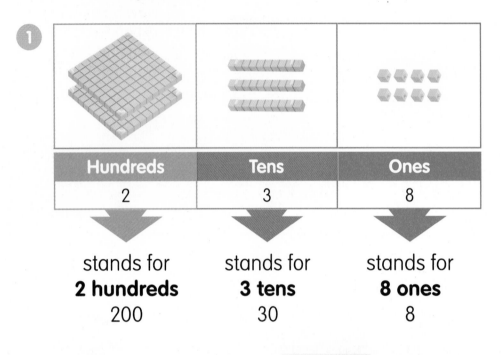

Hundreds	Tens	Ones
2	3	8

stands for **2 hundreds** 200

stands for **3 tens** 30

stands for **8 ones** 8

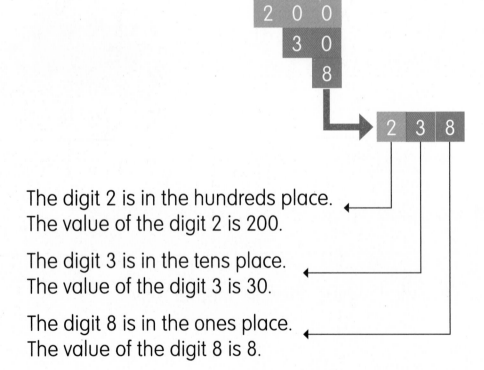

The digit 2 is in the hundreds place.
The value of the digit 2 is 200.

The digit 3 is in the tens place.
The value of the digit 3 is 30.

The digit 8 is in the ones place.
The value of the digit 8 is 8.

2 We can write numbers in different ways.

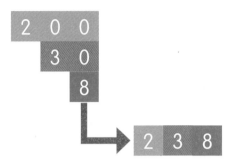

200, 30, and 8 make 238.

238 = 2 hundreds 3 tens 8 ones
    = 200 + 30 + 8

200 + 30 + 8 is the expanded form of 238.

238 is the standard form of 238.

We write 200 as two hundred.

We write 38 as thirty-eight.

Two hundred thirty-eight is the word form of 238.

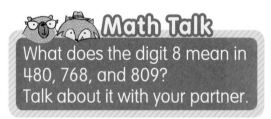

Math Talk

What does the digit 8 mean in 480, 768, and 809?
Talk about it with your partner.

Hands-on Activity Showing and writing numbers

Work in pairs.

① Use 1 2 3 to show these numbers.

a   473   b   204   c   840

② Write each number in expanded form and word form.
Then, circle the place value of the digit 4 for each number.

Number: 473

Expanded form: _____

Word form: _____

Place value of digit 4: ones / tens / hundreds

Number: 204

Expanded form: _____

Word form: _____

Place value of digit 4: ones / tens / hundreds

Number: 840

Expanded form: _____

Word form: _____

Place value of digit 4: ones / tens / hundreds

Practice reading, writing, and representing numbers to 1,000

Find each missing number.

1 a

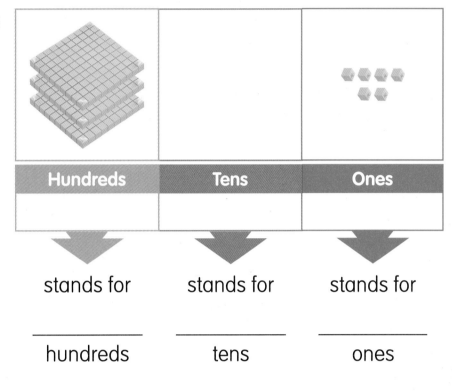

Hundreds	Tens	Ones

stands for   stands for   stands for

_____   _____   _____

hundreds   tens   ones

_____   _____   _____

3 0 6

b The digit _____ is in the hundreds place.

The value of the digit 3 is _____.

c The digit _____ is in the tens place.

The value of the digit 0 is _____.

d The digit _____ is in the ones place.

The value of the digit 6 is _____.

Fill in each blank.

2 | 9 | 1 | 5 |

_____ hundreds ←

_____ ten ←

_____ ones ←

3 139 = 1 hundred + _____ tens + 9 ones

= 100 + _____ + 9

4 768 = _____ hundreds + 6 tens + 8 ones

= _____ + 60 + 8

5 In 457,

| 4 | 5 | 7 |

the value of the digit 4 is _____. ←

the value of the digit 5 is _____. ←

the value of the digit 7 is _____. ←

Write each number in word form.

6 256 _____

7 380 _____

Write each number in standard form.

8 six hundred seven _____

9 five hundred thirteen _____

Write each number in expanded form.

10 471 = _____ + _____ + _____

11 809 = _____ + _____ + _____

Name: _____ Date: _____

INDEPENDENT PRACTICE

How many 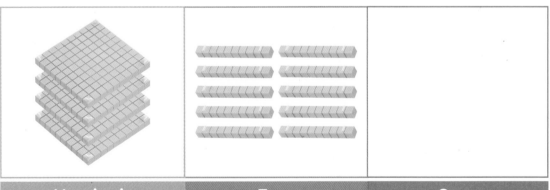 are there?
Write each number in expanded form, standard form, and word form.

1

Hundreds	Tens	Ones

Expanded form: _____

Standard form: _____

Word form: _____

2

Hundreds	Tens	Ones

Expanded form: _____

Standard form: _____

Word form: _____

Fill in each blank.

3 _____ + 80 + 6 = | 7 | 8 | 6 |

_____ hundreds ←

_____ tens ←

_____ ones ←

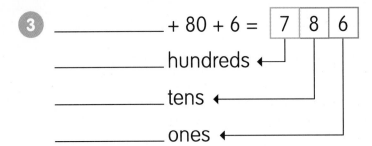

4 _____ + _____ = | 9 | 0 | 2 |

_____ hundreds ←

_____ tens ←

_____ ones ←

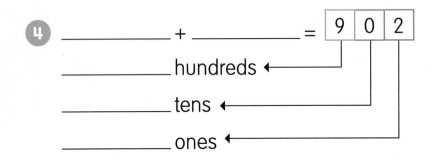

5 400 + 50 + 9 = | | | |

_____ hundreds ←

_____ tens ←

_____ ones ←

Read the clues to find the number.

6 I am a 3-digit number.

9 is in my hundreds place.

6 is in my ones place.

7 is in my tens place.

What number am I? _____

3 Comparing and Ordering Numbers

Learning Objectives:
- Use base-ten blocks and place-value charts to compare numbers.
- Compare numbers using the terms greater than and less than.
- Compare numbers using symbols < and >.
- Order 3-digit numbers.

THINK

Find each missing number.

a _____ more than 718 is 818.

b 526 less than _____ is 200.

Share how you find each missing number with your partner.

> Which number is greater?
> Which number is less?
> What do I need to find?

ENGAGE

1 Use [blocks] and a place-value chart to show 47 and 74.

Which is greater, 47 or 74?

How do you know?

2 Write down a 3-digit number less than 800.

Finish the sentence: _____ more than (your number) is 900.

3 Write down a 3-digit number less than 600.

Finish the sentence: _____ less than 700 is (your number).

LEARN Compare numbers

1 Which is greater, 235 or 126?

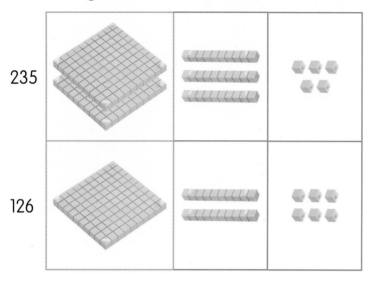

235

126

Compare the hundreds.
The hundreds are different.
2 hundreds are greater
than 1 hundred.

235 is greater than 126.
We can write 235 > 126.

2 Which is less, 242 or 215?

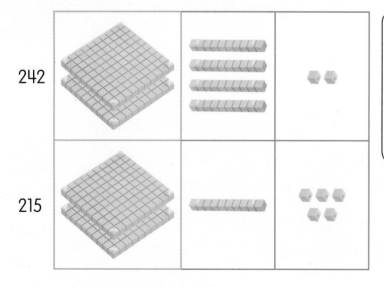

242

215

First, compare
the hundreds.
They are equal.
Then, compare the tens.
The tens are different.
1 ten is less than 4 tens.

215 is less than 242.
We can write 215 < 242.

3 Compare 418 and 415.
Which is greater?
Which is less?

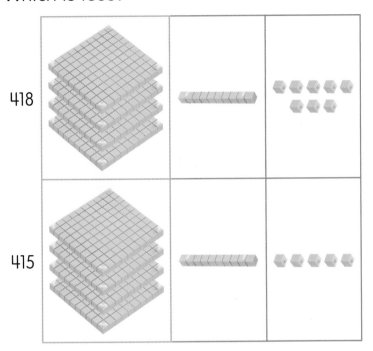

418		
415		

First, compare the hundreds.
The hundreds are equal.

Next, compare the tens.
The tens are equal.

Next, compare the ones.
The ones are different.
5 ones are less than
8 ones.

418 is greater than 415.
418 > 415
415 is less than 418.
415 < 418

Hands-on Activity Comparing numbers

Work in pairs.

① Use [▦] to show 103 and 113 to your partner.

Example:

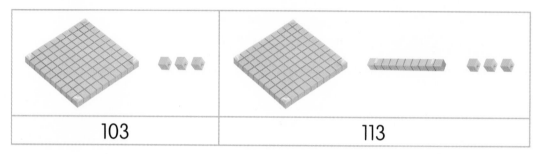

| 103 | 113 |

② Ask your partner to compare the numbers using greater than or less than aloud.

③ Trade places.
Repeat ① and ② with these numbers.

a   337 and 276

b   429 and 423

TRY Practice comparing numbers

Compare the numbers.
Fill in the blank with greater than or less than.

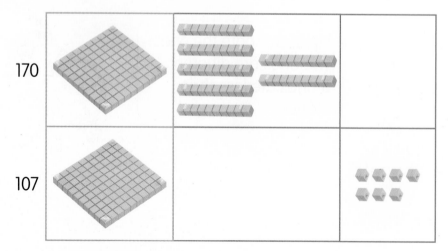

| 170 | | |
| 107 | | |

① 107 is _____ 170.

ENGAGE

1 Put 73, 71, and 80 in order:

   a   from least to greatest.

   b   from greatest to least.

2 Three numbers are ordered as shown.
What is a possible number for the blank?

628   630   _____

LEARN Compare and order three numbers

1 Arrange 489, 236, and 701 from least to greatest.

	Hundreds	Tens	Ones
489	4	8	9
236	2	3	6
701	7	0	1

Compare the hundreds.
7 hundreds are greater than 4 hundreds.
4 hundreds are greater than 2 hundreds.

701 is the greatest.
236 is the least.

From least to greatest, the numbers are:

236   489   701
least   greatest

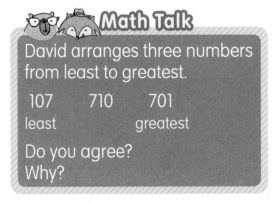

Math Talk

David arranges three numbers from least to greatest.

107   710   701
least   greatest

Do you agree?
Why?

Hands-on Activity Comparing and ordering three numbers

Work in pairs.

1. Use [1][2][3] to show these three numbers.

   274   247   427

2. Compare the numbers using greater than, less than, greatest, or least aloud.

3. Order the numbers from greatest to least.

   _____   _____   _____

     greatest   least

4. Trade places.
   Repeat ① to ③ with these numbers.

   742   782   757

   _____   _____   _____

     greatest   least

TRY Practice comparing and ordering three numbers

**Compare and order the numbers from greatest to least.
Fill in each blank.**

Hundreds	Tens	Ones
1	1	5
2	5	1
1	5	1

1. _____ is the greatest.

2. _____ is the least.

3. _____   _____   _____
     greatest   least

Name: _____   Date: _____

INDEPENDENT PRACTICE

Compare the numbers.
Fill in each blank with greater than or less than.

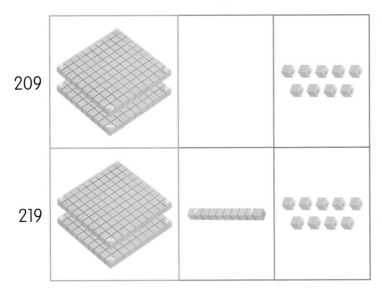

1 209 is _____ 219.

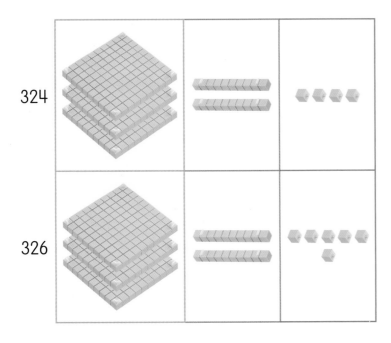

2 326 is _____ 324.

Compare the numbers.
Fill in the blank with greater than or less than.

3 55 is _____ 455.

Compare the numbers.
Write <, >, or =.

4 463 ◯ 430

Compare and order the numbers from greatest to least.
Fill in each blank.

Hundreds	Tens	Ones
9	1	2
9	2	1
2	9	1

5 _____ is the greatest.

6 _____ is the least.

7 _____ _____ _____
   greatest   least

Order the numbers from greatest to least.

8 683, 386, 863

   _____ _____ _____
   greatest   least

Order the numbers from least to greatest.

9 478, 874, 784

   _____ _____ _____
   least   greatest

4 Number Patterns

Learning Objective:
- Identify number patterns.

THINK

Alex writes three numbers.

275   285   270

Alex needs two other numbers to make a number pattern.
What are the two possible numbers?
How do you know?

How can I continue the pattern?
What do I need to find?

ENGAGE

1 Look at the number tape.

43	45	47	49	?

Compare the tens of the numbers.
What do you notice?
Then, compare the ones of the numbers.
What do you notice?
Now, find the missing number.
Talk about how you find your answer with your partner.

2 Write a set of five numbers to make a pattern.
Tell your partner how the pattern is made.

LEARN Find missing numbers in a number pattern

1 What is 10 more than 225?

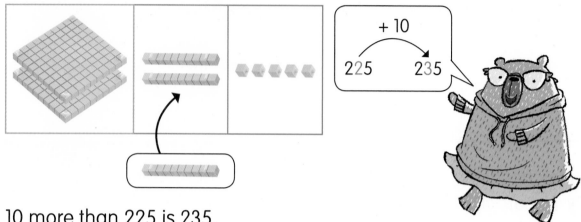

10 more than 225 is 235.

What is 10 less than 225?

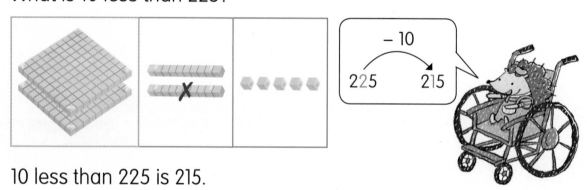

10 less than 225 is 215.

2 What is 10 more than 351?
What is 10 less than 401?

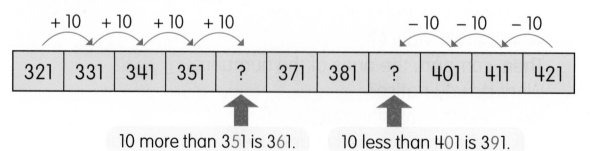

10 more than 351 is 361.   10 less than 401 is 391.

③ What is 100 more than 217?

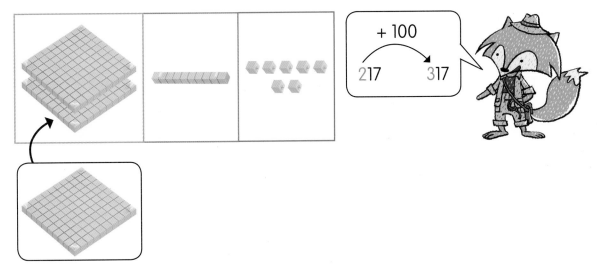

100 more than 217 is 317.

What is 100 less than 217?

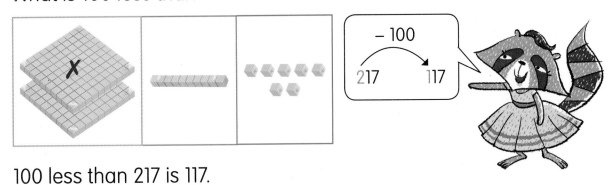

100 less than 217 is 117.

④ What is 100 more than 328?
What is 100 less than 828?

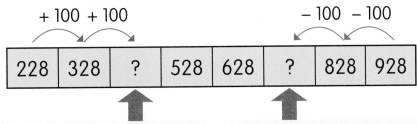

| 228 | 328 | ? | 528 | 628 | ? | 828 | 928 |

100 more than 328 is 428.   100 less than 828 is 728.

5 What is 5 more than 405?
What is 5 less than 430?

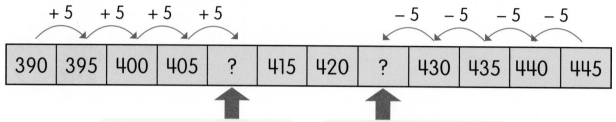

| 390 | 395 | 400 | 405 | ? | 415 | 420 | ? | 430 | 435 | 440 | 445 |

5 more than 405 is 410.   5 less than 430 is 425.

6 What comes next in the pattern?
200, 205, 210, 215, ?

220 comes next in
the pattern.

+5 +5 +5 +5
200, 205, 210, 215, 220

Hands-on Activity Making number patterns

Work in pairs.

1 Write eight numbers that make up a number pattern.
Use numbers greater than 100 but less than 1,000.

Example:

105   205   305   405   505   605   705   805

2 Replace any three of the numbers in ① with blanks.

Example:

105, 205, 305, _____, _____, 605, 705, _____

3 Ask your partner to fill in the blanks in ②.

TRY Practice finding missing numbers in a number pattern

Find each missing number.

1

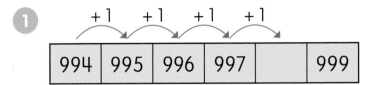

994	995	996	997		999

2

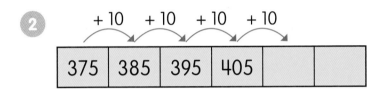

375	385	395	405		

3

400	500	600			900

With arrows: + 100 + 100 + 100 + 100

4 What is 5 less than 175? _____

5 What is 10 more than 274? _____

6 298, 299, 300, 301, 302, _____, 304, _____

7 342, 442, 542, 642, 742, _____, _____

Mathematical Habit 8 Look for patterns

The numbers are arranged in a pattern.

45	50	47	52	49	54	51	56	53	?	?	60

How can you find the missing numbers?

MATH SHARING

Lucas and Yong try to find how many numbers there are from 3 to 9.

They use different ways to find the answer.

I count the numbers.
3, 4, 5, 6, 7, 8, 9
There are 7 numbers from 3 to 9.

Lucas

I subtract the two numbers.
9 − 3 = 6

Yong

Lucas is correct.
Yong needs to add 1 more to the answer.

How many numbers are there from:

1 8 to 15?

2 22 to 38?

3 44 to 79?

Count to check your answers to 1, 2, and 3.

INDEPENDENT PRACTICE

Fill in each blank.

1 1 more than 205 is _____.

2 _____ is 2 less than 557.

3 10 more than 235 is _____.

4 10 less than 455 is _____.

5 What is 5 more than 145? _____.

6 What is 100 less than 347? _____.

Find each missing number.

7

105 | 106 | 107 | 108 | 109 |

8

137 | 140 | 143 | 146 | 149 |

9

250 | 245 | 240 | 235 | 230 |

10

390 | 380 | 370 | 360 | |

11

243 | 343 | 443 | 543 | |

12

| 525 | 522 | 519 | 516 |

13

| 805 | 815 | 825 | 835 |

14

| | 940 | 950 | 960 | 970

Mathematical Habit 8 Look for patterns

Make your own number pattern.
How did you do it?

Problem Solving with Heuristics

 Mathematical Habit 8 Look for patterns

The numbers make a pattern.
Draw arrows to show each number pattern.

a

b

2 **Mathematical Habit 1** **Persevere in solving problems**

Lilian and Ravi started counting at the same time.
Lilian counted on by tens from 300.
Ravi counted back by hundreds.
After six counts, they reached the same number.
What number did Ravi start counting back from?

CHAPTER WRAP-UP

How can you use a place-value chart to compare three numbers?

Numbers to 1,000

Counting to 1,000

Place Value

Comparing and Ordering Numbers

Number Patterns

3 hundreds
4 tens
6 ones

Standard form: 346
Word form: three hundred forty-six
Expanded form: 300 + 40 + 6

$+10 \quad +10 \quad +10$
548, 558, 568, 578

$-100 \quad -100 \quad -100$
834, 734, 634, 534

$+5 \quad +5 \quad +5$
905, 910, 915, 920

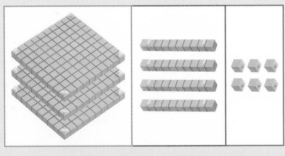

100, ..., 200, ..., 300, ..., 310, ..., 320, ..., 330, ..., 340, 341, 342, 343, 344, 345, 346

976   769   796
Order the numbers from greatest to least.

- Compare the hundreds. 976 is the greatest number.

- Compare the tens. 769 is the least number.

976   796   769
greatest   least

Name: _____ Date: _____

Count.
Fill in the blank.

 1

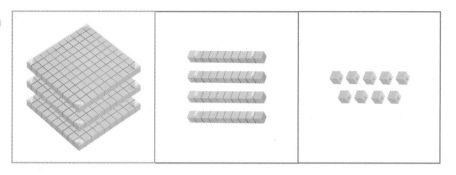

_____

Count on by ones, tens, or hundreds.
Find each missing number.

2 436 437 438 _____ _____ _____

3 405 505 605 _____ _____ _____

Find each missing number.

 4

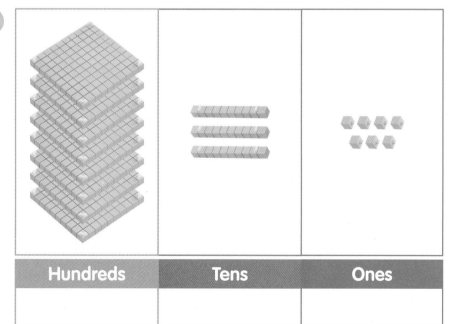

Hundreds	Tens	Ones

Write each number in word form.

5 212 _____

6 322 _____

Write each number in standard form.

7 four hundred forty _____

8 six hundred eight _____

Write each number in expanded form.

9 710 = _____

10 256 = _____

Compare the numbers.
Fill in the blank with greater than or less than.

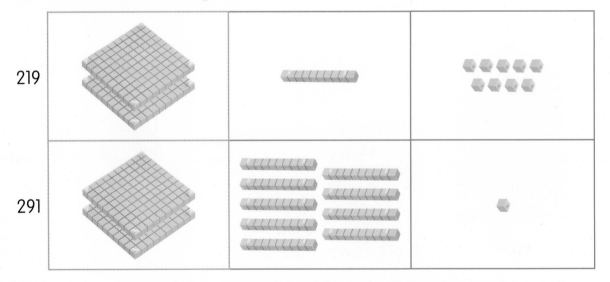

219		
291		

11 219 is _____ 291.

Compare the numbers.
Fill in each blank with greater than or less than.

12 482 is _____ 428.

13 656 is _____ 659.

Compare the numbers.
Fill in each blank with <, >, or =.

14 299 ◯ 399

15 516 ◯ 514

Compare and order the numbers from greatest to least.
Fill in each blank.

Hundreds	Tens	Ones
3	7	2
2	3	7
3	2	7

16 _____ is the greatest.

17 _____ is the least.

18 _____ _____ _____
     greatest   least

Order these numbers from least to greatest.

19 368, 386, 638

_____ _____ _____
    least   greatest

Order the numbers from greatest to least.

20 591, 519, 951

_____ _____ _____
greatest   least

Find each missing number.

21 _____ is 10 less than 418.

22 _____ is 100 more than 806.

The numbers are arranged in a pattern.
Find each missing number.

23 436, 437, 438, 439, _____, _____, _____

24 245, 255, 265, 275, _____, _____, _____

Assessment Prep

Answer each question.

25 Which number is less than 678?

(A) 687   (B) 618

(C) 688   (D) 686

26 Which number sentence is true?

(A) 370 < 307   (B) 832 < 823

(C) 148 = 184   (D) 490 > 486

Name: _____ Date: _____

Numbers and Patterns

1 Natalie is thinking of a number.
The number has 5 hundreds, 9 tens, and 3 ones.
Write the number in standard form and word form.
Use the place-value chart to help you.

Hundreds	Tens	Ones

Standard form: _____

Word form: _____

The value of the digit 9 is _____.

2 a Complete the number pattern.

191   201   211   221   251

b How did you find each missing number?

Draw pictures or use  to help you.

3 **a**　Order the numbers from greatest to least.
752, 932, 751

_____ _____ _____
　　greatest　　　　　　　　　　　least

b　How did you find the answer to **a**?
Explain your answer.

4　James is bouncing a basketball.
He counts on by hundreds for each bounce.
He starts counting at 400 and ends at 900.
How many times does he bounce the ball?
Explain your answer.

Rubric

Point(s)	Level	My Performance
7–8	4	• Most of my answers are correct. • I show all my work correctly. • I explain my thinking clearly and completely.
5–6.5	3	• Some of my answers are correct. • I show some of my work correctly. • I explain my thinking clearly.
3–4.5	2	• A few of my answers are correct. • I show little work correctly. • I explain some of my thinking clearly.
0–2.5	1	• A few of my answers are correct. • I show little or no work. • I do not explain my thinking clearly.

Teacher's Comments

STEAM

Spotted Turtles

Have you ever seen a "polka-dot" turtle?
Its whole body is sprinkled with yellow spots.
The number of spots on a spotted turtle
changes over time.
A baby spotted turtle may have only one spot on
its shell.
When it is a grown-up, it may have about 100 spots.

Task

A Turtle Wall

Work in groups.

1. Visit the library to learn about spotted turtles.
   Write a report or a story about them.

2. Use black and yellow crayons to draw a
   spotted turtle on a large sheet of art paper.

3. Cut out your turtle.
   Count and write the number of spots on the
   back of the picture.

4. Have the class count the spots on your turtle.
   Check their answers.

5. Put the turtles together on a wall.
   As a class, count as far as you can all of
   the spots.

6. Add your report or story to the wall.
   Take turns reading your work aloud.

What are the ways that you can add numbers within 1,000?

Name: _____ Date: _____

Adding mentally

a 34 + 2 = ?

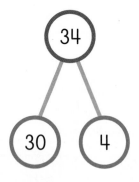

4 + 2 = 6
30 + 6 = 36
So, 34 + 2 = 36.

b 65 + 30 = ?

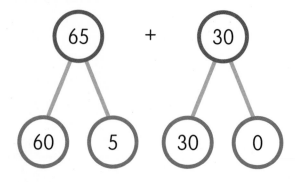

60 + 30 = 90
5 + 0 = 5
90 + 5 = 95
So, 65 + 30 = 95.

▶ **Quick Check**

Add mentally.

① 46 + 3 = _____

② 78 + 20 = _____

Adding three numbers

5 + 8 + 4 = ?

STEP 1 Make 10.
5 + 5 = 10

STEP 2 10 + 3 = 13

STEP 3 13 + 4 = 17

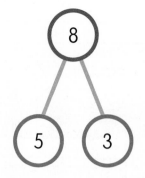

So, 5 + 8 + 4 = 17.

▶ **Quick Check**

Add.

③ 3 + 6 + 5 = _____

④ 6 + 9 + 2 = _____

Adding without regrouping

62 + 5 = ?

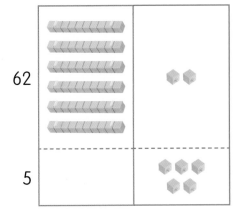

62

5

Step 1
Add the ones.

	Tens	Ones
	6	2
+		5
		7

2 ones + 5 ones
= 7 ones

Step 2
Add the tens.

	Tens	Ones
	6	2
+		5
	6	7

6 tens + 0 tens
= 6 tens

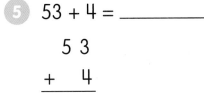

So, 62 + 5 = 67.

▶ **Quick Check**

⑤ 53 + 4 = _____

    5 3
+   4
_____

⑥ 82 + 7 = _____

    8 2
+   7
_____

Adding with regrouping

54 + 8 = ?

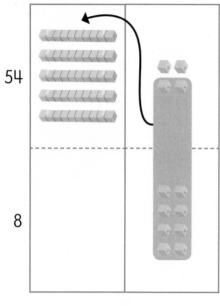

54

8

Step 1
Add the ones.

	Tens	Ones
	5	4
+		8
		2

4 ones + 8 ones
= 12 ones

Regroup the ones.
12 ones = 1 ten 2 ones

Step 2
Add the tens.

	Tens	Ones
	5	4
+		8
	6	2

1 ten + 5 tens + 0 tens
= 6 tens

So, 54 + 8 = 62.

▶ **Quick Check**

7 63 + 9 = _____

    6 3
+   9
_____

8 78 + 7 = _____

    7 8
+   7
_____

1 Adding Fluently Within 100

Learning Objectives:
- Add numbers within 20 mentally using different strategies.
- Use addition strategies and algorithm to add numbers within 100.

THINK

Find the missing digit.

```
    2   8
+   3   ?
_____
    6   3
```

Share the steps to find the missing digit with your partner.

ENGAGE

1. Use your fingers to count on from 14 to 18.
   How many fingers did you need?

2. Jayden counted on from a number to 16.
   He counted and raised 4 fingers.
   What number did he start from?

LEARN Add mentally within 20

1. Find 16 + 3.
   Count on by ones from 16.

16	17	18	19

   So, 16 + 3 = 19.

   This is another way to add.

   16 + 3 = 19

   (10) (6)

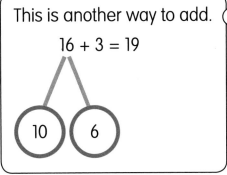

2 Find 8 + 6.

8 + 6 = ?

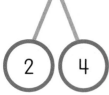

8 + 2 = 10

10 + 4 = 14

So, 8 + 6 = 14.

First, make 10.
Then, add 4 to 10.

3 Find 5 + 7.

5 + 7 = ?

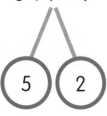

5 + 7 = 5 + 5 + 2

     = 10 + 2

     = 12

So, 5 + 7 = 12.

You can use doubles fact of 5 + 5 to add 5 and 7.

TRY Practice adding mentally within 20

Add mentally.

1. $16 + 2 =$ _____

2. $4 + 15 =$ _____

3. $10 + 3 =$ _____

4. $4 + 7 =$ _____

5. $7 + 7 =$ _____

6. $8 + 9 =$ _____

7. $6 + 9 =$ _____

8. $5 + 6 =$ _____

Mathematical Habit 2 Use mathematical reasoning

Add 5 and 9 mentally.
What are the methods you can use to add?
Share with your partner the method that you use to add.
Use the method to add 6 and 7.

MATH SHARING

ENGAGE

1 Add 12 to 34 using a place-value chart.

2 Hannah adds 12 to another number and gets 49.

_____ + 12 = 49

What is the number?

LEARN Add within 100 without regrouping

1 41 + 23 = ?

Step 1
Add the ones.

	4	1
+	2	3
		4

1 one + 3 ones
= 4 ones

Step 2
Add the tens.

	4	1
+	2	3
	6	4

4 tens + 2 tens
= 6 tens

So, 41 + 23 = 64.

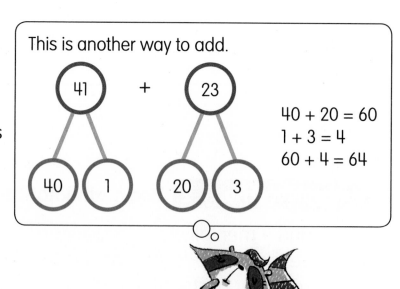

This is another way to add.

41 + 23

40 1   20 3

40 + 20 = 60
1 + 3 = 4
60 + 4 = 64

TRY Practice adding within 100 without regrouping

Add.

1.
```
   2 4
 + 1 2
 _____
```

2.
```
   4 3
 + 3 5
 _____
```

3.
```
   5 6
 + 2 1
 _____
```

4.
```
   1 3
 + 7 4
 _____
```

5.
```
   4 2
 + 4 7
 _____
```

6.
```
   3 0
 + 6 4
 _____
```

Add.
Show your work.

7. 45 + 14 = _____

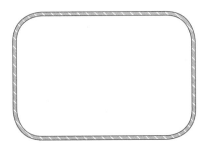

8. 76 + 23 = _____

9. 19 + 60 = _____

10. 27 + 61 = _____

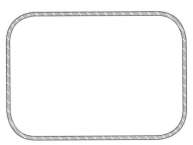

ENGAGE

1 Use the make 10 strategy to add 7 and 5.

2 What number is added to 28 to make 55?

Finish the addition sentence: 28 + _____ = 55.

LEARN Add within 100 with regrouping

1 Add 46 and 39.

Step 1
Add the ones.

```
   1
   4  6
+  3  9
      5
```

6 ones + 9 ones
= 15 ones

Regroup the ones.
15 ones = 1 ten 5 ones

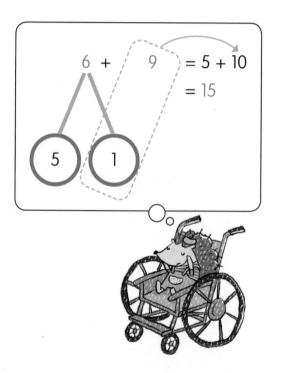

6 + 9 = 5 + 10
= 15

5   1

Step 2
Add the tens.

```
   1
   4  6
+  3  9
   8  5
```

1 ten + 4 tens + 3 tens
= 8 tens

So, 46 + 39 = 85.

Work in pairs.

(1) Choose two numbers from 10 to 50.

(2) Add the numbers.

Tens   Ones

+

(3) Ask your partner to check your work.

(4) Trade places. Repeat (1) to (3) again.

Tens   Ones

+

TRY Practice adding within 100 with regrouping

Add.

(1) 27 + 16 = _____

      2 7
    + 1 6
    _____

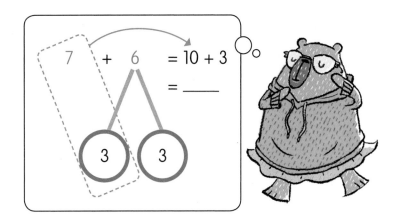

7 + 6 = 10 + 3
            = ____

3   3

2 45 + 29 = _____

$$
\begin{array}{r}
4\ 5 \\
+\ 2\ 9 \\
\hline
\end{array}
$$

3 13 + 68 = _____

$$
\begin{array}{r}
1\ 3 \\
+\ 6\ 8 \\
\hline
\end{array}
$$

Add.
Show your work.

4 39 + 17 = _____

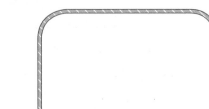

5 38 + 37 = _____

6 25 + 58 = _____

7 18 + 74 = _____

MATH SHARING

Mathematical Habit 7 Make use of structure

Jacob wrote these number sentences.

$5 + 9 = 9 + 5$
$16 + 4 = 4 + 16$
$58 + 27 = 27 + 58$

Are the number sentences true?
Can you think of others?
Share them with your partner.

ENGAGE

1 Draw number bonds to help you add.

   a   9 + 6   **b**   7 + 8

   Talk about how you find your answers with your partner.

2 How do you find 39 + 6, 47 + 8, and 7 + 58?
   Talk about how you find your answers with your partner.

LEARN Add mentally within 100

1   58 + 8 = ?

8 and 2 make 10.

   STEP 1   Add 10 to 58.
   58 + 10 = 68

   STEP 2   Subtract 2 from 68.
   68 − 2 = 66

   So, 58 + 8 = 66.

TRY Practice adding mentally within 100

Add mentally.

1   38 + 6 = _____

2   45 + 7 = _____

3   76 + 9 = _____

4   87 + 8 = _____

ADD MENTALLY

What you need:

Players: 2
Materials: Mental addition cards

What to do:

Place the deck of mental addition cards face down.

1 Player 1 turns over a card.

2 Player 2 adds the numbers on the card.

3 Player 1 checks the answer.
Player 2 gets a point if the answer is correct.

4 Trade places. Repeat 1 to 3.

Who is the winner?

The player with more points after 5 rounds wins.

INDEPENDENT PRACTICE

Add mentally.

1 $13 + 2 =$ _____

2 $2 + 17 =$ _____

3 $8 + 4 =$ _____

4 $3 + 9 =$ _____

5 $7 + 9 =$ _____

6 $8 + 8 =$ _____

7 $8 + 5 =$ _____

8 $6 + 6 =$ _____

Add.

9
$$\begin{array}{r} 7\ 2 \\ +\ 1\ 4 \\ \hline \end{array}$$

10
$$\begin{array}{r} 4\ 7 \\ +\ 5\ 1 \\ \hline \end{array}$$

11
$$\begin{array}{r} 3\ 7 \\ +\ 2\ 5 \\ \hline \end{array}$$

12
$$\begin{array}{r} 1\ 4 \\ +\ 6\ 8 \\ \hline \end{array}$$

Add.
Show your work.

13) 55 + 24 = _____

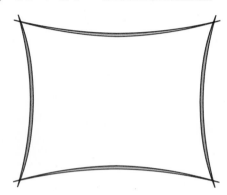

14) 13 + 82 = _____

15) 69 + 26 = _____

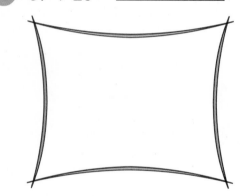

16) 36 + 57 = _____

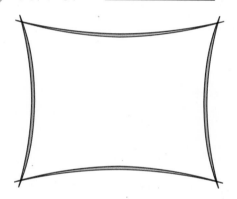

Add mentally.

17) 29 + 5 = _____

18) 36 + 7 = _____

19) 47 + 7 = _____

20) 54 + 9 = _____

21) 65 + 8 = _____

22) 85 + 6 = _____

2 Adding Without Regrouping

Learning Objective:
- Use addition strategies and algorithm to add up to 3-digit numbers without regrouping.

 THINK

Find the missing digits.

$$
\begin{array}{ccc}
  & 2 & 4 & 6 \\
+ & ? & ? & ? \\
\hline
  & 6 & 7 & 8
\end{array}
$$

Share the steps to find the missing digits with your partner.

ENGAGE

Use counting tape to add.

a   24 + 3   b   24 + 30   c   24 + 300

Then, use the counting tape to find 25 + 43.
Share how you add with your partner.

LEARN Add within 1,000 without regrouping

1 Add 163 and 4.
   Count on by ones from 163.

| **163** | 164 | 165 | 166 | 167 |

So, 163 + 4 = 167.

This is another way to add.

163 + 4 = 167

160   3

2 Find the value of 254 + 30.
Count on by tens from 254.

254	264	274	284

So, 254 + 30 = 284.

3 368 + 200 = ?
Count on by hundreds from 368.

368	468	568

So, 368 + 200 = 568.

Are there other ways to add?

Math Talk

How do you add these mentally?
a 167 + 2
b 167 + 20
c 167 + 200

4 There are 871 adults and 27 children at a concert.
How many people are at the concert?
Add 871 and 27 to find out.

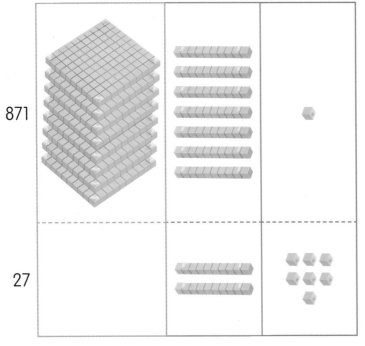

Step 1
Add the ones.

	8	7	1
+		2	7
			8

1 one + 7 ones
= 8 ones

Step 2
Add the tens.

	8	7	1
+		2	7
		9	8

7 tens + 2 tens
= 9 tens

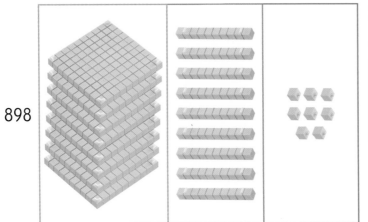

Step 3
Add the hundreds.

	8	7	1
+		2	7
	8	9	8

8 hundreds +
0 hundreds
= 8 hundreds

So, 871 + 27 = 898.
898 people are at the concert.

5 Find the value of 145 + 112.

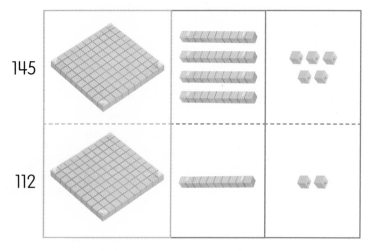

145

112

257

So, 145 + 112 = 257.

Step 1
Add the ones.

	1	4	5
+	1	1	2
			7

5 ones + 2 ones
= 7 ones

Step 2
Add the tens.

	1	4	5
+	1	1	2
		5	7

4 tens + 1 ten
= 5 tens

Step 3
Add the hundreds.

	1	4	5
+	1	1	2
	2	5	7

1 hundred +
1 hundred
= 2 hundreds

Work in pairs.

1. Add 312 and 237.
   Show your work.

Hundreds	Tens	Ones
☐	☐	☐
+ ☐	☐	☐
☐	☐	☐

2. Ask your partner to use [blocks] to check your work.

3. Trade places. Repeat ① and ② with these numbers.

   a 972 + 24

Hundreds	Tens	Ones
☐	☐	☐
+ ☐	☐	☐
☐	☐	☐

   b 142 + 507

Hundreds	Tens	Ones
☐	☐	☐
+ ☐	☐	☐
☐	☐	☐

TRY Practice adding within 1,000 without regrouping

Add mentally.

① 153 + 4 = _____

② 153 + 40 = _____

③ 153 + 400 = _____

Add.

④ 213 + 21 = ?

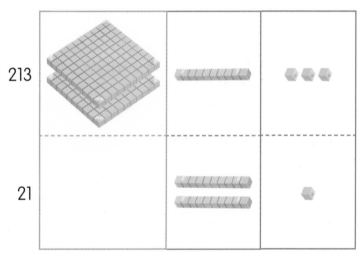

First, add the ones.
Next, add the tens.
Then, add the hundreds.

So, 213 + 21 = _____ .

```
    2 1 3
  +   2 1
  _____
```

Add.

⑤
```
    2 3 6
  +   4 1
  _____
```

⑥
```
    6 4 5
  + 1 2 1
  _____
```

INDEPENDENT PRACTICE

Add mentally.

1 $181 + 3 =$ _____

2 $762 + 20 =$ _____

3 $846 + 100 =$ _____

Add.

4
$$\begin{array}{r} 1\,2\,4 \\ +\quad 2\,0 \\ \hline \end{array}$$

5
$$\begin{array}{r} 7\,9 \\ +\,8\,2\,0 \\ \hline \end{array}$$

6
$$\begin{array}{r} 4\,2\,1 \\ +\,1\,6\,4 \\ \hline \end{array}$$

7
$$\begin{array}{r} 7\,6\,3 \\ +\,1\,3\,2 \\ \hline \end{array}$$

8
$$\begin{array}{r} 2\,5\,3 \\ +\,5\,4\,1 \\ \hline \end{array}$$

9
$$\begin{array}{r} 1\,5\,2 \\ +\,8\,0\,6 \\ \hline \end{array}$$

Add.
Show your work.

10 741 + 18 = _____

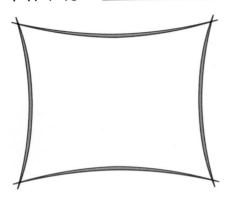

11 15 + 860 = _____

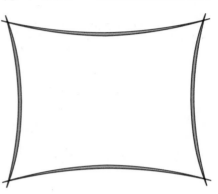

12 364 + 205 = _____

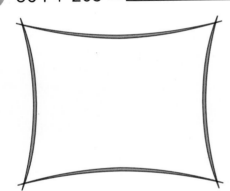

13 431 + 215 = _____

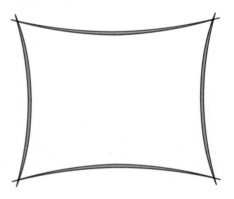

14 322 + 453 = _____

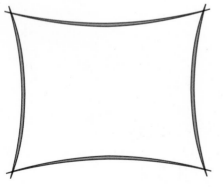

15 566 + 413 = _____

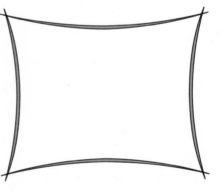

 3 Adding with Regrouping in Ones

Learning Objective:
• Use addition strategies and algorithm to add up to 3-digit numbers with regrouping in ones.

THINK

Find the missing digits.

```
    2  7  5
  + 1 [?][?]
  ─────────
    3  9  2
```

Share the steps to find the missing digits with your partner.

ENGAGE

1 Use the make 10 strategy to add 6 and 725.

2 How can you find the missing number?

634 + _____ = 643

LEARN Add within 1,000 with regrouping in ones

1 Lucia has 215 blue beads and 126 green beads.
How many beads does Lucia have in all?
Add 215 and 126 to find out.

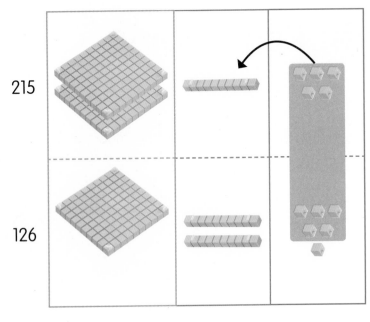

215

126

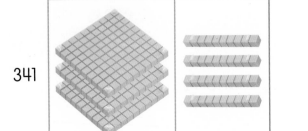

341

Step 1
Add the ones.

	1		
	2	1	5
+	1	2	6
			1

5 ones + 6 ones = 11 ones

Regroup the ones.
11 ones = 1 ten 1 one

Step 2
Add the tens.

	1		
	2	1	5
+	1	2	6
		4	1

1 ten + 1 ten + 2 tens = 4 tens

Step 3
Add the hundreds.

	1		
	2	1	5
+	1	2	6
	3	4	1

2 hundreds + 1 hundred = 3 hundreds

So, 215 + 126 = 341.
Lucia has 341 beads in all.

Math Talk

Why is this addition incorrect?

357
+ 138
485

Explain to your partner the correct way to add.

Work in pairs.

① Add 619 and 203.
Show your work.

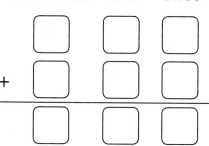

② Ask your partner to use 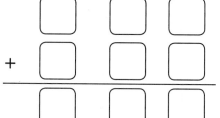 to check your work.

③ Trade places. Repeat ① and ② with these numbers.

a   357 + 18

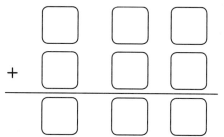

b   403 + 358

Hundreds Tens Ones

TRY Practice adding within 1,000 with regrouping in ones

Add.

① 157 + 35 = ?

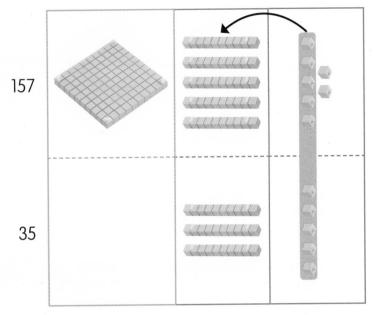

157

35

First, add the ones.
Regroup the ones into tens and ones.
Next, add the tens.
Then, add the hundreds.

So, 157 + 35 = _____ .

$$
\begin{array}{r}
1\ 5\ 7 \\
+\ \ \ 3\ 5 \\
\hline
\end{array}
$$

 **Math Talk**

Jason adds 139 and 24 this way.

$$
\begin{array}{r}
139 \\
+\ \ 24 \\
\hline
1513
\end{array}
$$

Why is his answer incorrect?
Share the correct way to add with your partner.

Add.

2
```
  1 3 6
+   2 7
```

3
```
    3 5
+ 6 4 5
```

4
```
  4 2 9
+ 4 3 6
```

5
```
  2 7 4
+ 7 0 6
```

Add.
Show your work.

6 408 + 45 = _____

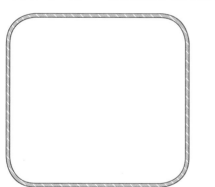

7 53 + 919 = _____

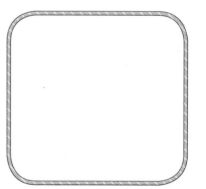

8 634 + 259 = _____

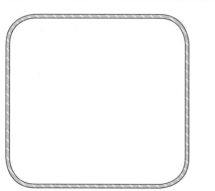

9 128 + 857 = _____

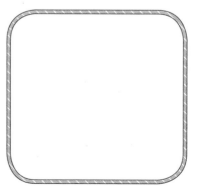

ENGAGE

1 Draw number bonds to find each missing number.

a $9 +$ _____ $= 10$ **b** $8 +$ _____ $= 10$ **c** $7 +$ _____ $= 10$

Complete: Adding _____ is the same as adding 10 and subtracting _____.

2 How can you use the addition sentences in **1** to add 126 and 7?

LEARN Add ones to a 3-digit number mentally

1 $134 + 7 = ?$

STEP **1** Add 6 to 134.
$134 + 6 = 140$

STEP **2** Add 1 to the result.
$140 + 1 = 141$

So, $134 + 7 = 141$.

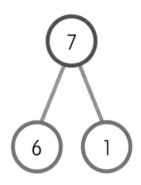

2 $347 + 8 = ?$

STEP **1** Add 10 to 347.
$347 + 10 = 357$

STEP **2** Subtract 2 from the result.
$357 - 2 = 355$

So, $347 + 8 = 355$.

8 and 2 make 10.

TRY Practice adding ones to a 3-digit number mentally

Add mentally.

1 $173 + 9 =$ _____

2 $287 + 8 =$ _____

3 $6 + 325 =$ _____

4 $9 + 468 =$ _____

Name: _____   Date: _____

INDEPENDENT PRACTICE

Bryson is looking for his football.
The number on his football is less than 783 but greater than 694.
Which is his ball?
Add to find out.
Then, circle your answer.

1

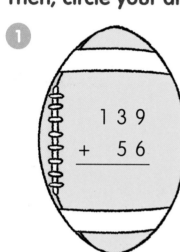

139
+ 56

408
+ 23

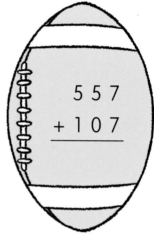

557
+107

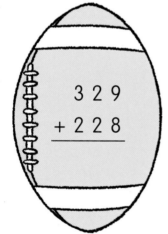

329
+228

66
+806

309
+471

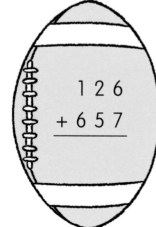

126
+657

255
+636

717
+279

Add.
Show your work.

2 447 + 46 = _____

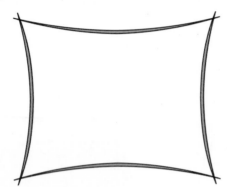

3 162 + 219 = _____

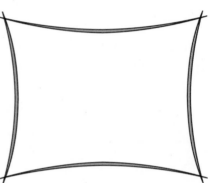

4 579 + 204 = _____

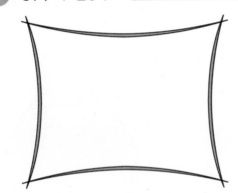

5 639 + 321 = _____

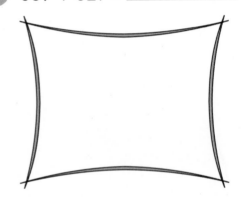

Add mentally.

6 242 + 9 = _____

7 456 + 7 = _____

8 539 + 6 = _____

9 724 + 8 = _____

10 875 + 7 = _____

11 913 + 9 = _____

Adding with Regrouping in Tens

Learning Objective:
• Use addition strategies and algorithm to add up to 3-digit numbers with regrouping in tens.

THINK

Find the missing digits.

```
    2  7  4
 +  1 [?][?]
 ──────────
    4  5  9
```

Share the steps to find the missing digits with your partner.

ENGAGE

1. Add each pair of numbers.
   a   150 and 70   b   80 and 190
   How did you add the numbers?

2. Use the method in ① to add 162 and 80.
   Tell your partner the steps you took to add.

3. Use the method in ① to find the missing number in the
   sentence: 175 + _____ = 258.

LEARN Add within 1,000 with regrouping in tens

1. There are 182 adults and 193 children at a game.
   How many people are there at the game?
   Add 182 and 193 to find out.

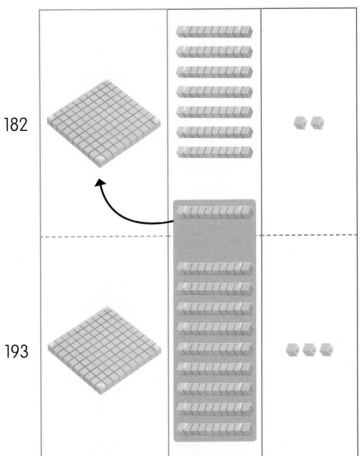

Step 1
Add the ones.

	1	8	2
+	1	9	3
			5

2 ones + 3 ones
= 5 ones

Step 2
Add the tens.

	1		
	1	8	2
+	1	9	3
		7	5

8 tens + 9 tens
= 17 tens

Regroup the tens.
17 tens = 1 hundred 7 tens

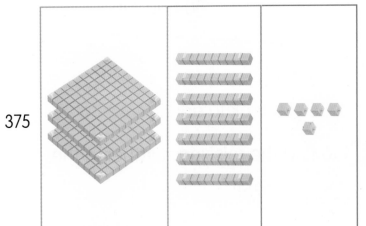

Step 3
Add the hundreds.

	1		
	1	8	2
+	1	9	3
	3	7	5

1 hundred +
1 hundred +
1 hundred
= 3 hundreds

So, 182 + 193 = 375.
There are 375 people at the game.

Work in pairs.

① Add 423 and 394.
Show your work.

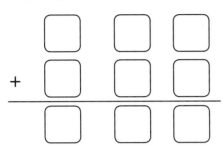

② Ask your partner to use 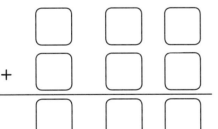 to check your work.

③ Trade places. Repeat ① and ② with these numbers.

a   583 + 56

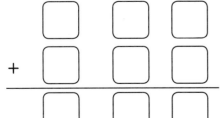

b   694 + 214

Hundreds   Tens   Ones

TRY Practice adding within 1,000 with regrouping in tens

Add.

1 174 + 82 = ?

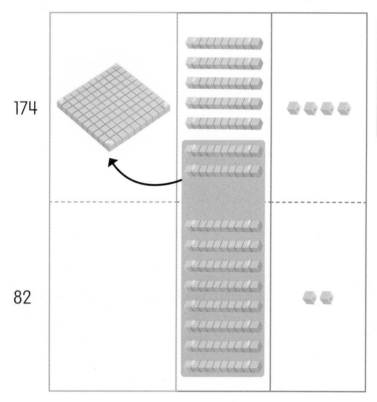

174

82

First, add the ones.
Next, add the tens.
Regroup the tens into hundreds and tens.
Then, add the hundreds.

So, 174 + 82 = _____.

```
  1 7 4
+   8 2
```

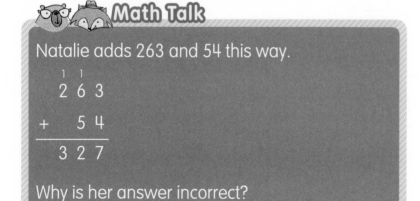

Math Talk

Natalie adds 263 and 54 this way.

```
  1 1
  2 6 3
+   5 4
───────
  3 2 7
```

Why is her answer incorrect?
Share the correct way to add with your partner.

Add.

2
```
  5 4 9
+   9 0
```

3
```
    5 5
+ 7 6 2
```

4
```
  4 6 3
+ 1 8 6
```

5
```
  1 4 2
+ 7 7 2
```

Add.
Show your work.

6 453 + 75 = _____

7 61 + 648 = _____

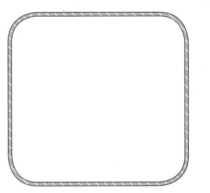

8 332 + 296 = _____

9 280 + 549 = _____

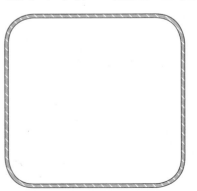

ENGAGE

1 Draw number bonds to find each missing number.

a 90 + _____ = 100   **b** 80 + _____ = 100   **c** 70 + _____ = 100

Complete: Adding _____ is the same as adding 100 and subtracting _____.

2 How can you use the addition sentences in **1** to add 196 and 70?

LEARN Add tens to a 3-digit number mentally

1 134 + 90 = ?

STEP **1** Make 100.
90 + 10 = 100

STEP **2** Add 124 to 100.
100 + 124 = 224

So, 134 + 90 = 224.

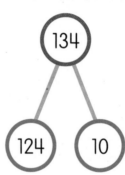

2 345 + 80 = ?

STEP **1** Add 100 to 345.
345 + 100 = 445

STEP **2** Subtract 20 from the result.
445 − 20 = 425

So, 345 + 80 = 425.

20 and 80 make 100.

TRY Practice adding tens to a 3-digit number mentally

Add mentally.

1 247 + 80 = _____

2 351 + 90 = _____

3 468 + 70 = _____

4 795 + 60 = _____

INDEPENDENT PRACTICE

Briella is looking for her helmet.
The number on her helmet is greater than 807 but less than 919.
Which is her helmet?
Add to find out.
Then, circle your answer.

1

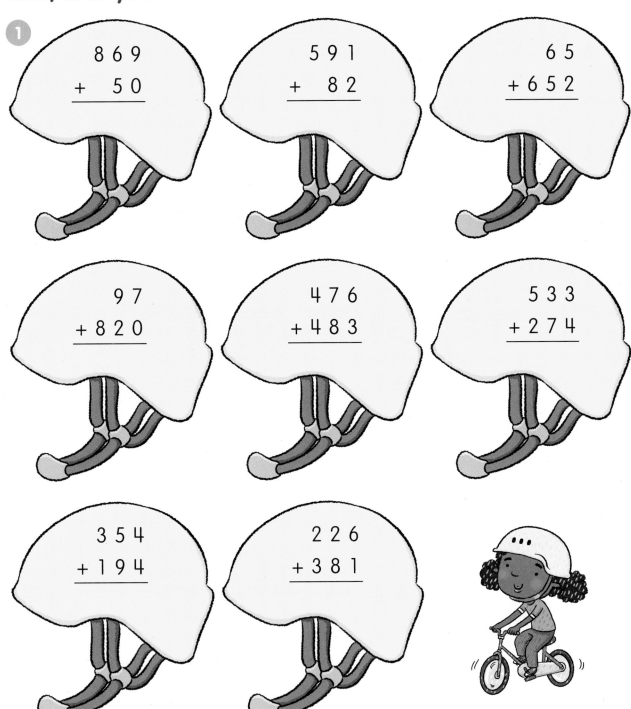

```
  8 6 9        5 9 1         6 5
+   5 0      +   8 2       + 6 5 2
```

```
  9 7         4 7 6         5 3 3
+ 8 2 0      + 4 8 3       + 2 7 4
```

```
  3 5 4        2 2 6
+ 1 9 4      + 3 8 1
```

Add.
Show your work.

2 345 + 180 = _____

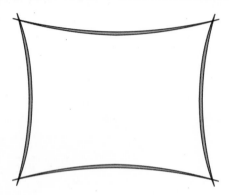

3 167 + 461 = _____

4 582 + 173 = _____

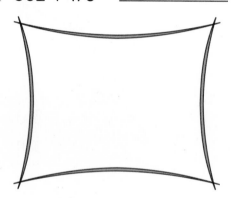

5 618 + 291 = _____

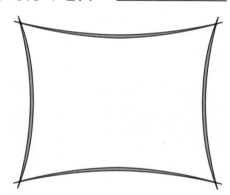

Add mentally.

6 354 + 70 = _____

7 567 + 60 = _____

8 628 + 90 = _____

9 765 + 80 = _____

10 859 + 60 = _____

11 872 + 90 = _____

5 Adding with Regrouping in Ones and Tens

Learning Objective:
• Use addition strategies and algorithm to add up to 3-digit numbers with regrouping in ones and tens.

THINK

Find the missing digits.

```
    4  8  [?]
 +  2 [?]  6
 ─────────────
    7  0  1
```

Share the steps to find the missing digits with your partner.

ENGAGE

1 Regroup to add.

    a   68 + 7   **b**   68 + 57

2 Find the missing number in the addition sentence:

867 + _____ = 916.

Tell your partner how you regrouped to add.

LEARN Add within 1,000 with regrouping in ones and tens

1 There are 278 blue markers and 386 black markers in a box.
How many markers are there in the box?
Add 278 and 386 to find out.

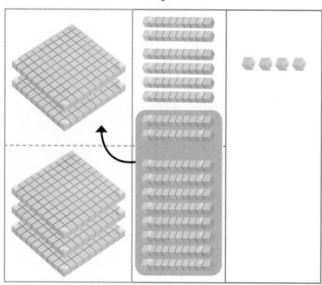

Step 1
Add the ones.

		1	
	2	7	8
+	3	8	6
			4

8 ones + 6 ones = 14 ones

Regroup the ones.
14 ones = 1 ten 4 ones

Step 2
Add the tens.

	1	1	
	2	7	8
+	3	8	6
		6	4

1 ten + 7 tens + 8 tens = 16 tens

Regroup the tens.
16 tens = 1 hundred 6 tens

Step 3
Add the hundreds.

	1	1	
	2	7	8
+	3	8	6
	6	6	4

1 hundred + 2 hundreds + 3 hundreds = 6 hundreds

So, 278 + 386 = 664.
There are 664 markers in the box.

Work in pairs.

① Add 443 and 479.
Show your work.

	Hundreds	Tens	Ones
	◻	◻	◻
+	◻	◻	◻
	◻	◻	◻

② Ask your partner to use 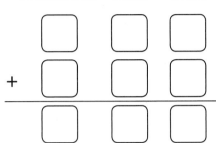 to check your work.

③ Trade places. Repeat ① and ② with these numbers.

a   568 + 97

	Hundreds	Tens	Ones
	◻	◻	◻
+	◻	◻	◻
	◻	◻	◻

b   387 + 423

	Hundreds	Tens	Ones
	◻	◻	◻
+	◻	◻	◻
	◻	◻	◻

TRY Practice adding within 1,000 with regrouping in ones and tens

1 288 + 23 = ?

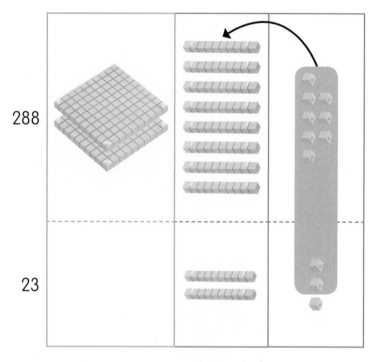

288

23

First, add the ones.
Regroup the ones into tens and ones.
Next, add the tens.
Regroup the tens into hundreds and tens.
Then, add the hundreds.

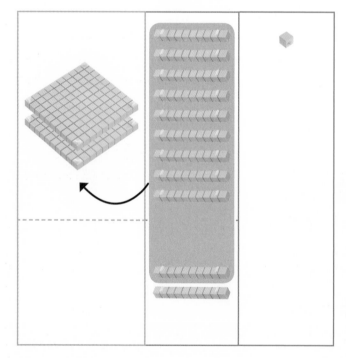

```
   2 8 8
 +   2 3
```

So, 288 + 23 = _____.

Add.

2
```
  2 7 5
+   8 7
———————
```

3
```
    5 2
+ 7 6 8
———————
```

4
```
  4 6 4
+ 2 8 9
———————
```

5
```
  1 5 3
+ 4 4 9
———————
```

Add.
Show your work.

6 109 + 99 = _____

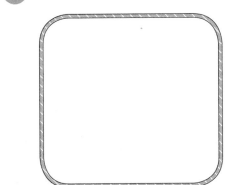

7 87 + 138 = _____

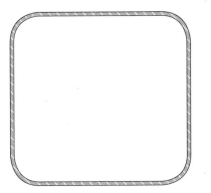

8 473 + 398 = _____

9 564 + 358 = _____

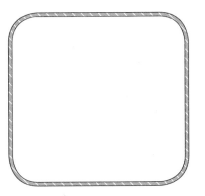

ENGAGE

How does making 100 help you add 98 and 5?
Draw a number bond to show your thinking.
Try again with 97 and 5.
Did you do it the same way?
Share your thinking with your partner.

LEARN Add tens and ones mentally

1 99 + 2 = ?

STEP 1 Make 100.
99 + 1 = 100

STEP 2 Add 100 to 1.
100 + 1 = 101

So, 99 + 2 = 101.

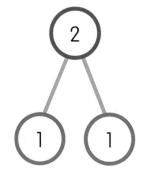

2 216 + 98 = ?

STEP 1 Make 100.
98 + 2 = 100

STEP 2 Add 100 to 214.
214 + 100 = 314

So, 216 + 98 = 314.

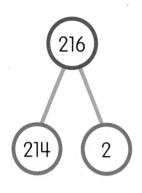

TRY Practice adding tens and ones mentally

Add mentally.

1 96 + 7 = _____

2 329 + 97 = _____

INDEPENDENT PRACTICE

Add.
Then, match.

1

$$\begin{array}{r} 5\ 6 \\ +\ 2\ 5\ 7 \\ \hline \end{array}$$

$$\begin{array}{r} 1\ 9\ 9 \\ +\ \ \ 9\ 9 \\ \hline \end{array}$$

 700

721

 313

$$\begin{array}{r} 8\ 9\ 5 \\ +\ \ \ 2\ 8 \\ \hline \end{array}$$

$$\begin{array}{r} 4\ 0\ 3 \\ +\ 2\ 9\ 7 \\ \hline \end{array}$$

 712

923

 298

$$\begin{array}{r} 2\ 4\ 5 \\ +\ 4\ 6\ 7 \\ \hline \end{array}$$

$$\begin{array}{r} 4\ 8\ 8 \\ +\ 2\ 3\ 3 \\ \hline \end{array}$$

Add.
Show your work.

2 809 + 99 = _____

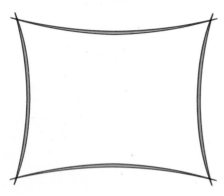

3 595 + 127 = _____

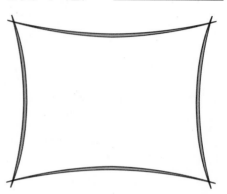

4 689 + 121 = _____

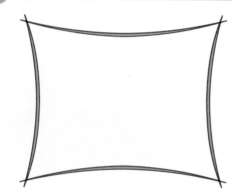

5 677 + 223 = _____

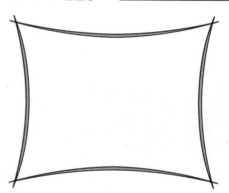

Add mentally.

6 98 + 8 = _____

7 99 + 6 = _____

8 97 + 5 = _____

9 345 + 96 = _____

10 583 + 98 = _____

11 768 + 99 = _____

6 Adding Four 2-Digit Numbers

Learning Objective:
• Use addition strategies and algorithm to add up to four 2-digit numbers.

THINK

Find the missing number.

54 + 28 + 36 + _____ = 129

Talk about how you can find the missing number with your partner.

ENGAGE

Show how you add 11, 14, and 17 in two different ways.

LEARN Add three 2-digit numbers

1 Find 19 + 34 + 21.

Step 1
Add the ones.

```
  1
  1 9
  3 4
+ 2 1
    4
```

9 ones + 4 ones + 1 one
= 14 ones

Regroup 14 ones.
14 ones = 1 ten 4 ones

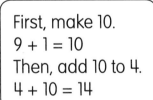

First, make 10.
9 + 1 = 10
Then, add 10 to 4.
4 + 10 = 14

Step 2
Add the tens.

```
  1
  1 9
  3 4
+ 2 1
  7 4
```

1 ten + 1 ten + 3 tens + 2 tens
= 7 tens

So, 19 + 34 + 21 = 74.

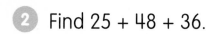

2 Find 25 + 48 + 36.

Step 1
Add the ones.

```
    1
    2  5
    4  8
 +  3  6
       9
```

5 ones + 8 ones + 6 ones
= 19 ones

Regroup 19 ones.
19 ones = 1 ten 9 ones

First, add the top two digits.
5 + 8 = 13
Then, add 13 to 6.
6 + 13 = 19

Step 2
Add the tens.

```
 1     1
    2  5
    4  8
 +  3  6
 1  0  9
```

1 ten + 2 tens + 4 tens + 3 tens
= 10 tens

Regroup 10 tens.
10 tens = 1 hundred 0 tens

So, 25 + 48 + 36 = 109.

TRY Practice adding three 2-digit numbers

Add.

1
```
    1 4
    3 0
 +  2 3
```

2
```
    4 3
    1 7
 +  2 6
```

3
```
    5 8
    4 1
 +  1 3
```

4
```
    2 9
    3 3
 +  5 6
```

ENGAGE

Show how you add 21, 34, 12, and 23 in two or more different ways.
Think of another four 2-digit numbers.
Trade your numbers with your partner and add them.

LEARN Add four 2-digit numbers

1 Find 22 + 13 + 37 + 15.

Step 1
Add the ones.

```
  1
  2 2
  1 3
  3 7
+ 1 5
      7
```

2 ones + 3 ones +
7 ones + 5 ones
= 17 ones

Regroup 17 ones.
17 ones = 1 ten 7 ones

First, add the top two digits.
2 + 3 = 5
Next, use doubles fact.
5 + 5 = 10
Then, add 10 to 7.
7 + 10 = 17

Step 2
Add the tens.

```
  1
  2 2
  1 3
  3 7
+ 1 5
  8 7
```

1 ten + 2 tens + 1 ten + 3 tens + 1 ten
= 8 tens

So, 22 + 13 + 37 + 15 = 87.

Math Talk
What other ways can you add 22 + 13 + 37 + 15 mentally?

2 Find 45 + 16 + 21 + 52.

Step 1
Add the ones.

```
  1
    4 5
    1 6
    2 1
+   5 2
      4
```

5 ones + 6 ones
+ 1 one + 2 ones
= 14 ones

Regroup 14 ones.
14 ones = 1 ten 4 ones

First, add the top
two digits.
5 + 6 = 11
Next, add the bottom
two digits.
1 + 2 = 3
Then, add 11 and 3.
11 + 3 = 14

Step 2
Add the tens.

```
  1   1
    4 5
    1 6
    2 1
+   5 2
  1 3 4
```

1 ten + 4 tens + 1 ten + 2 tens + 5 tens
= 13 tens

Regroup 13 tens.
13 tens = 1 hundred 3 tens

So, 45 + 16 + 21 + 52 = 134.

TRY Practice adding four 2-digit numbers

Add.

1
```
    1 3
    2 4
    4 7
+   1 2
```

2
```
    3 4
    4 2
    1 5
+   5 7
```

INDEPENDENT PRACTICE

Add.

1
```
   4 0
   1 6
 + 3 2
-------
```

2
```
   2 8
   5 2
 + 1 7
-------
```

3
```
   4 7
   2 4
 + 3 2
-------
```

4
```
   1 5
   7 9
 + 2 3
-------
```

Add.
Show your work.

5 25 + 41 + 20 = _____

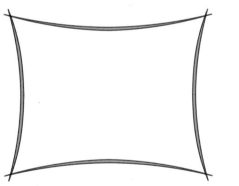

6 36 + 23 + 34 = _____

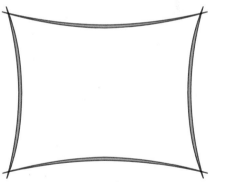

7 47 + 32 + 26 = _____

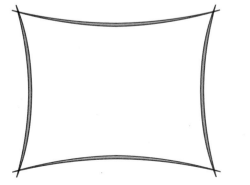

8 29 + 15 + 62 = _____

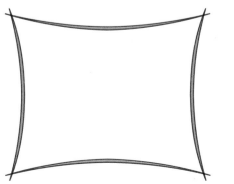

Add.

9
```
   2 4
   1 2
   3 2
 + 2 1
```

10
```
   1 5
   2 1
   2 3
 + 3 6
```

11
```
   2 5
   1 5
   5 3
 + 2 3
```

12
```
   3 1
   4 3
   4 5
 + 1 8
```

Add.
Show your work.

13 $25 + 31 + 12 + 20 = $ _____

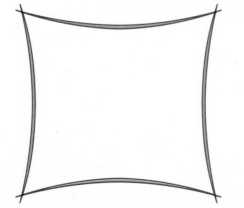

14 $15 + 22 + 11 + 47 = $ _____

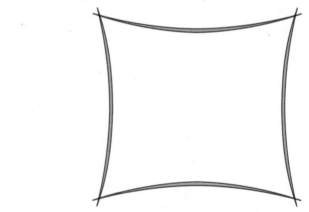

15 $38 + 13 + 14 + 41 = $ _____

16 $53 + 24 + 25 + 32 = $ _____

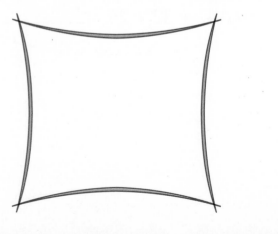

Mathematical Habit 3 Construct viable arguments

The answer in the example is incorrect.
Spot the mistake.
Then, write the correct working.

```
    1 7 8
  + 3 8 4
  ───────
    5 5 2
```

Problem Solving with Heuristics

1 **Mathematical Habit 1** **Persevere in solving problems**

Make two 3-digit numbers from the numbers below.
Use each number once.
What are the two 3-digit numbers that give the greatest answer
when you add them?

| 3 | 5 | 2 | 4 | 1 | 0 |

Which two numbers
can you add to get the
greatest hundreds?

2 **Mathematical Habit 1** **Persevere in solving problems**

Find each missing number.

There is more than one answer.

```
    4 ? 3
+   2 8 4
─────────
    7 ? 7
```

CHAPTER WRAP-UP

Addition Within 1,000

Adding Mentally

a counting on
$16 + 2 = 18$

16	17	18	19

b making 10
$9 + 3 = 9 + 1 + 2$
$\quad\quad\ = 10 + 2$
$\quad\quad\ = 12$

c using a doubles fact
$6 + 8 = 6 + 6 + 2$
$\quad\quad\ = 14$

d $67 + 8 = ?$

STEP 1 Add 10.
$67 + 10 = 77$

STEP 2 Subtract 2 from the result.
$77 - 2 = 75$

e $123 + 8 = ?$

STEP 1 Add 7 to 123.
$123 + 7 = 130$

STEP 2 Add 1 to the result.
$130 + 1 = 131$

f $131 + 80 = ?$

STEP 1 Make 100.
$80 + 20 = 100$

STEP 2 Add 111 to the result.
$100 + 111 = 211$

Adding 3-Digit Numbers

a Add without regrouping
Step 1 Add the ones.
Step 2 Add the tens.
Step 3 Add the hundreds.

	1	4	5
+	1	1	2
	2	5	7

b Add with regrouping
Step 1 Add the ones.
Regroup the ones.
Step 2 Add the tens.
Regroup the tens.
Step 3 Add the hundreds.

	1	1	
	3	5	8
+	2	6	4
	6	2	2

Adding Four 2-Digit Numbers

You can add the digits in each place value by first adding the top two digits. Next, add the bottom two digits. Then, add both the results.

	4	2
	1	2
	1	3
+	2	1
	8	8

Name: _____ Date: _____

Add mentally.

1. 14 + 2 = _____

2. 4 + 15 = _____

3. 9 + 4 = _____

4. 3 + 8 = _____

5. 5 + 5 = _____

6. 8 + 7 = _____

7. 5 + 9 = _____

8. 7 + 6 = _____

Add.

9.
```
    2 6
  + 1 3
  _____
```

10.
```
    3 9
  + 5 9
  _____
```

Add.
Show your work.

11. 38 + 31 = _____

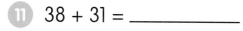
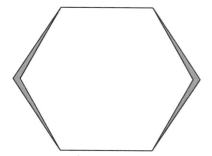

12. 18 + 76 = _____

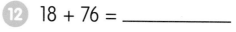

Add mentally.

13. 37 + 8 = _____

14. 56 + 9 = _____

15. 66 + 7 = _____

16. 78 + 5 = _____

Add.

17
```
   6 6 2
 + 2 1 4
```

18
```
   4 6 5
 + 1 1 9
```

19
```
   4 6 5
 + 3 4 2
```

20
```
   7 1 4
 + 1 9 6
```

Add.
Show your work.

21 463 + 135 = _____

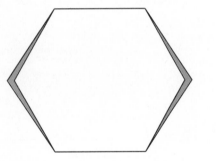

22 437 + 356 = _____

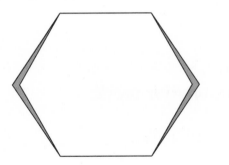

23 282 + 544 = _____

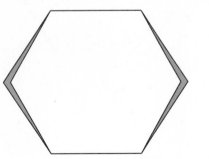

24 234 + 667 = _____

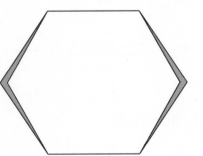

Add mentally.

25 273 + 4 = _____

26 541 + 30 = _____

27 429 + 200 = _____

28 657 + 8 = _____

29 736 + 80 = _____

30 864 + 97 = _____

Add.

31
```
   5 3
   3 1
 + 1 3
```

32
```
   1 8
   5 6
 + 3 4
```

33
```
   2 2
   1 1
   4 3
 + 1 0
```

34
```
   4 7
   3 1
   1 5
 + 2 4
```

Add.
Show your work.

35 23 + 34 + 69 = _____

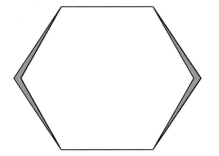

36 38 + 43 + 42 + 26 = _____

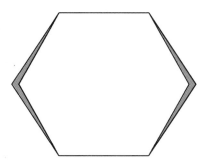

Assessment Prep

Answer each question.

37 Which of the following gives the answer 234?
Make a ✓ in the correct circle.

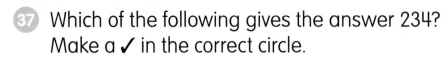

○	○	○
187 + 123	68 + 166	70 + 164

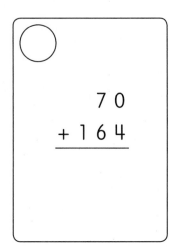

○	○	○
160 + 74	205 + 84	100 + 134

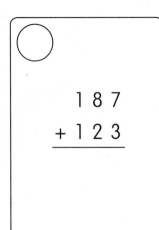
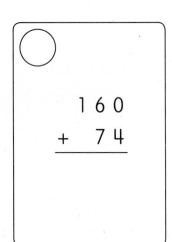
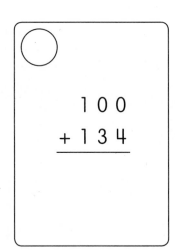

38 What is the missing number?

```
  4 ☐
+ 2 3
─────
  7 2
```

Name: _____ Date: _____

At the Library

1 Find each missing number.

a
```
    4   6
 +  3  [ ]
 ─────────
    7   9
```

b
```
    1  [ ]  2
 +      2   3
 ──────────────
    1   9   5
```

c
```
    1  [ ]  5
 +  1   1   4
 ──────────────
    3   0   9
```

2 A librarian buys 68 Spanish books and 121 English books.
How many books does the librarian buy in all?
Show your work.

68 + 121 = _____

The librarian buys _____ books in all.

3 Kwan's class borrowed 37 storybooks.
There were 54 storybooks left.
How many storybooks were there at first?
Show your work.

37 + 54 = _____

There were _____ storybooks at first.

4 Two boxes of books were donated to the school library.
There were 325 books in all.
Which two boxes were donated to the school?
Show your work.

Box A

Box B

Box C

_____ and _____ were donated to the school.

Rubric

Point(s)	Level	My Performance
7–8	4	• Most of my answers are correct. • I show all my work correctly. • I explain my thinking clearly and completely.
5–6.5	3	• Some of my answers are correct. • I show some of my work correctly. • I explain my thinking clearly.
3–4.5	2	• A few of my answers are correct. • I show little work correctly. • I explain some of my thinking clearly.
0–2.5	1	• A few of my answers are correct. • I show little or no work. • I do not explain my thinking clearly.

Teacher's Comments

Subtraction Within 1,000

A nine hundred-legged bug, Millie, has lost some shoes.
She has only 864 shoes on her.
Help her find how many shoes she has lost.

How can we subtract two 3-digit numbers?

What are the ways that you can subtract numbers within 1,000?

Name: _____ Date: _____

Subtracting mentally

a   59 – 5 = ?

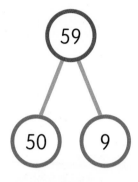

9 – 5 = 4
50 + 4 = 54

So, 59 – 5 = 54.

b   72 – 20 = ?

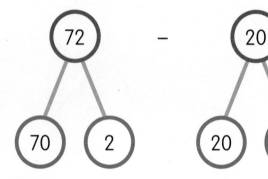

70 – 20 = 50
2 – 0 = 2
50 + 2 = 52

So, 72 – 20 = 52.

▶ **Quick Check**

Subtract mentally.

1   67 – 5 = _____

2   93 – 30 = _____

Subtracting without regrouping

48 − 6 = ?

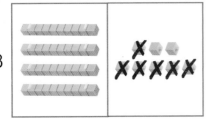

Step 1
Subtract the ones.

	Tens	Ones
	4	8
−		6
		2

8 ones − 6 ones
= 2 ones

Step 2
Subtract the tens.

	Tens	Ones
	4	8
−		6
	4	2

4 tens − 0 tens
= 4 tens

So, 48 − 6 = 42.

▶ **Quick Check**

Subtract.

③
```
   3 7
 −   6
```

④
```
   6 5
 −   3
```

⑤
```
   8 9
 −   4
```

⑥
```
   9 6
 −   5
```

Subtracting with regrouping

54 – 8 = ?

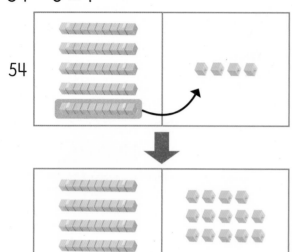

Step 1

Regroup the tens and ones.
Regroup the tens in 54.

54 = 5 tens 4 ones
    = 4 tens 14 ones

	Tens	Ones
	$\overset{4}{\cancel{5}}$	$\overset{14}{\cancel{4}}$
–		8

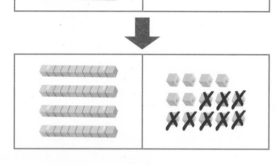

Step 2

Subtract the ones.

	Tens	Ones
	$\overset{4}{\cancel{5}}$	$\overset{14}{\cancel{4}}$
–		8
		6

14 ones – 8 ones
= 6 ones

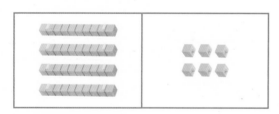

Step 3

Subtract the tens.

	Tens	Ones
	$\overset{4}{\cancel{5}}$	$\overset{14}{\cancel{4}}$
–		8
	4	6

4 tens – 0 tens
= 4 tens

So, 54 – 8 = 46.

▶ **Quick Check**

7

$$\begin{array}{r} 4\,2 \\ -5 \\ \hline \end{array}$$

8

$$\begin{array}{r} 8\,6 \\ -9 \\ \hline \end{array}$$

Subtracting Fluently Within 100

Learning Objectives:
- Subtract numbers within 20 mentally using different strategies.
- Use subtraction strategies and algorithm to subtract numbers within 100.

New Vocabulary
subtract mentally

THINK

Find the missing digit.

```
    7  4
 -  3 [?]
 _____
    3  5
```

Share the steps to find the missing digit with your partner.

ENGAGE

1 Use your fingers to count back from 16 to 12.
How many fingers did you need?

2 Find the missing number in the sentence: 18 – _____ = 13.

 **Subtract mentally within 20**

1 18 – 2 = ?
Count back by ones from 18.

13	14	15	16	17	**18**

So, 18 – 2 = 16.

This is another way to subtract.

18 – 2 = 16

10   8

2 Find 13 – 6.

$$13 - 6 = ?$$

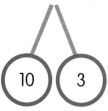

(10)   (3)

10 – 6 = 4
3 + 4 = 7

So, 13 – 6 = 7.

First, subtract 6 from 10.
Then, add 3 and 4.

3 Find 15 – 8.

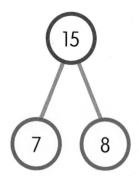

(15)

(7)   (8)

8 + 7 = 15
So, 15 – 8 = 7.

8 + 7 = 15 is the
related addition fact.

Work in pairs.
Your teacher will provide you with a bag of small items.

① Pick one item from the bag.

② Think of a story using the item that you pick.
Use the name of two friends and numbers smaller than 20.

③ Show the story with an addition or a subtraction sentence.

Example:
Pedro has 8 crayons.
Ava gives him 9 crayons.
Pedro has 17 crayons altogether.
$8 + 9 = 17$
$9 + 8 = 17$

Example:
Luna has 17 buttons.
There are 8 blue buttons.
There are 9 red buttons.
$17 - 8 = 9$
$17 - 9 = 8$

Your story:

Addition or subtraction sentence:

TRY Practice subtracting mentally within 20

Subtract mentally.

① $17 - 3 = $ _____

② $12 - 2 = $ _____

③ $11 - 7 = $ _____

④ $14 - 9 = $ _____

ENGAGE

1 What are the steps you take to subtract 2 tens and 3 ones from 58?

2 Describe the steps you take to subtract 34 from 67 to your partner.

LEARN Subtract within 100 without regrouping

1 35 – 4 = ?

Count back by ones from 35.

31	32	33	34	**35**

So, 35 – 4 = 31.

2 57 – 30 = ?

Count back by tens from 57.

27	37	47	**57**

So, 57 – 30 = 27.

3 Subtract 25 from 78.

```
    7 8
  – 2 5
      3
```

Step 1
Subtract the ones.
8 ones – 5 ones
= 3 ones

```
    7 8
  – 2 5
    5 3
```

Step 2
Subtract the tens.
7 tens – 2 tens
= 5 tens

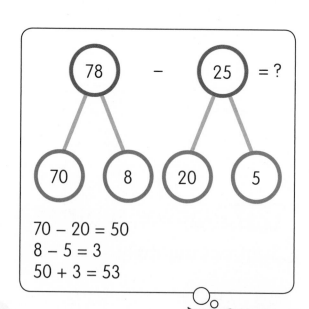

78 – 25 = ?

70   8   20   5

70 – 20 = 50
8 – 5 = 3
50 + 3 = 53

Check
```
    5 3
  + 2 5
    7 8
```

So, 78 – 25 = 53.

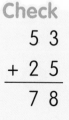

TRY Practice subtracting within 100 without regrouping

Count back to subtract.

1 68 − 3 = _____

2 95 − 4 = _____

3 74 − 30 = _____

4 82 − 40 = _____

Subtract.

5
```
   4 8
 − 2 3
```

6
```
   6 7
 − 5 4
```

7
```
   7 9
 − 3 6
```

8
```
   9 6
 − 4 5
```

**Subtract.
Show your work.**

9 56 − 32 = _____

10 78 − 16 = _____

11 84 − 41 = _____

12 95 − 74 = _____

ENGAGE

1 Regroup each number into tens and ones.

    a   37 = 2 tens _____ ones   **b**   46 = _____ tens 16 ones

2 Find two possible sets of numbers to make the sentence true.

    _____ = _____ tens 25 ones

LEARN Subtract within 100 with regrouping

1 Subtract 37 from 65.

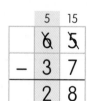

Step 1
Regroup the tens and ones.
Regroup the tens in 65.

    65 = 6 tens 5 ones
        = 5 tens 15 ones

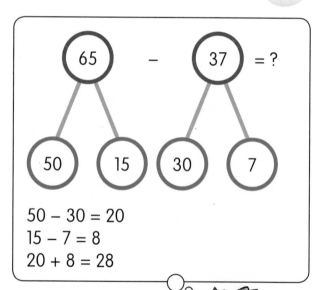

$$65 - 37 = ?$$

$$50 - 30 = 20$$
$$15 - 7 = 8$$
$$20 + 8 = 28$$

Step 2
Subtract the ones.
15 ones – 7 ones
= 8 ones

Step 3
Subtract the tens.
5 tens – 3 tens
= 2 tens

So, 65 – 37 = 28.

Check

```
    1
    2 8
  + 3 7
  -----
    6 5
```

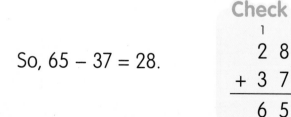

TRY Practice subtracting within 100 with regrouping

Subtract.

1.
```
   5 5
 - 2 8
```

2.
```
   8 2
 - 3 9
```

ENGAGE

1. Draw number bonds to find each missing number.

   a $10 - \underline{\hspace{1cm}} = 8$ b $10 - \underline{\hspace{1cm}} = 7$ c $10 - \underline{\hspace{1cm}} = 9$

2. How can you use the subtraction sentences in **1** to find each of the following?

   a $15 - 9 = \underline{\hspace{2cm}}$ b $20 - 7 = \underline{\hspace{2cm}}$

LEARN Subtract mentally within 100

1. $32 - 8 = ?$

   STEP 1 Subtract 10 from 32.
   $32 - 10 = 22$

   STEP 2 Add 2 to the result.
   $22 + 2 = 24$

   So, $32 - 8 = 24$.

8 and 2 make 10.

TRY Practice subtracting mentally within 100

Subtract mentally.

1. $28 - 9 = \underline{\hspace{2cm}}$

2. $32 - 5 = \underline{\hspace{2cm}}$

3. $53 - 6 = \underline{\hspace{2cm}}$

4. $86 - 7 = \underline{\hspace{2cm}}$

SUBTRACT MENTALLY

What you need:

Players: 2
Materials: Mental subtraction cards

What to do:

Place the deck of mental subtraction cards face down.

1. Player 1 turns over a card.
2. Player 2 subtracts the numbers on the card.
3. Player 1 checks the answer.
   Player 2 gets a point if the answer is correct.
4. Trade places. Repeat 1 to 3.

Who is the winner?

The player with more points after 5 rounds wins.

INDEPENDENT PRACTICE

Subtract mentally.

1 13 – 2 = _____

2 17 – 5 = _____

3 12 – 7 = _____

4 16 – 9 = _____

5 11 – 3 = _____

6 13 – 4 = _____

7 56 – 2 = _____

8 87 – 40 = _____

Subtract.

9
```
    6 7
  – 3 5
  ─────
```

10
```
    4 6
  – 2 1
  ─────
```

11
```
    8 9
  – 5 3
  ─────
```

12
```
    5 2
  – 1 9
  ─────
```

13
```
    6 4
  – 2 7
  ─────
```

14
```
    7 3
  – 4 5
  ─────
```

Subtract.
Show your work.

15 38 – 16 = _____

16 57 – 32 = _____

17 85 – 51 = _____

18 46 – 18 = _____

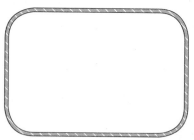

19 71 – 29 = _____

20 83 – 64 = _____

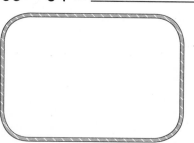

Subtract mentally.

21 27 – 8 = _____

22 34 – 6 = _____

23 42 – 7 = _____

24 68 – 9 = _____

25 75 – 6 = _____

26 93 – 7 = _____

© 2020 Marshall Cavendish Education Pte Ltd

2 Subtracting Without Regrouping

Learning Objective:
- Use subtraction strategies and algorithm to subtract up to 3-digit numbers without regrouping.

THINK

How do you find each missing digit?

$$
\begin{array}{ccc}
 & 7 & 8 & 5 \\
- & \boxed{?} & \boxed{?} & \boxed{?} \\
\hline
 & 4 & 1 & 2
\end{array}
$$

Share the steps to find the missing digits with your partner.

ENGAGE

1 Use  to show 347.
Count back to subtract each of the following.

   a 347 – 2   **b** 347 – 20   **c** 347 – 200

2 Use the same method to subtract the following.

   a 576 – 34   **b** 576 – 234

Share how you find your answers with your partner.

LEARN Subtract within 1,000 without regrouping

1 324 − 2 = ?

Count back by ones from 324.

322	323	**324**

So, 324 − 2 = 322.

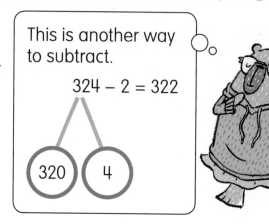

This is another way to subtract.

324 − 2 = 322

320   4

2 567 − 40 = ?

Count back by tens from 567.

527	537	547	557	**567**

So, 567 − 40 = 527.

3 718 − 300 = ?

Count back by hundreds from 718.

418	518	618	**718**

So, 718 − 300 = 418.

Are there other ways to subtract?

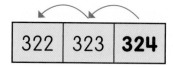 **Math Talk**

How do you subtract these mentally?
a 568 − 3
b 568 − 30
c 568 − 300

④ There were 137 apples at a fruit stall.
25 apples were sold.
How many apples were left?
Subtract 25 from 137 to find out.

137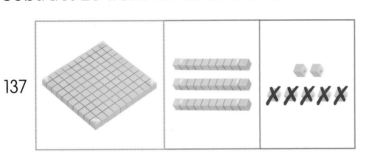

Step 1
Subtract the ones.

	1	3	7
−		2	5
			2

7 ones − 5 ones
= 2 ones

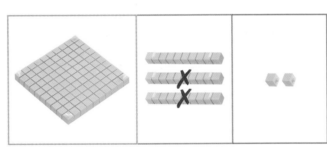

Step 2
Subtract the tens.

	1	3	7
−		2	5
		1	2

3 tens − 2 tens
= 1 ten

112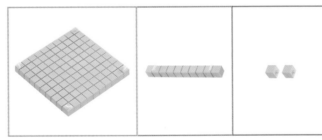

Step 3
Subtract the hundreds.

	1	3	7
−		2	5
	1	1	2

1 hundred
− 0 hundreds
= 1 hundred

Check

	1	1	2
+		2	5
	1	3	7

So, 137 − 25 = 112.
112 apples were left.

5 Subtract 124 from 249.

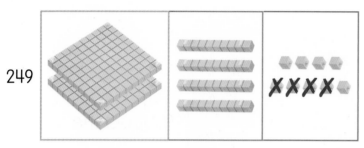

249

Step 1
Subtract the ones.

	2	4	9
−	1	2	4
			5

9 ones − 4 ones
= 5 ones

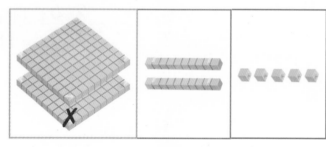

Step 2
Subtract the tens.

	2	4	9
−	1	2	4
		2	5

4 tens − 2 tens
= 2 tens

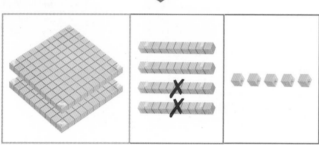

Step 3
Subtract the hundreds.

	2	4	9
−	1	2	4
	1	2	5

2 hundreds
− 1 hundred
= 1 hundred

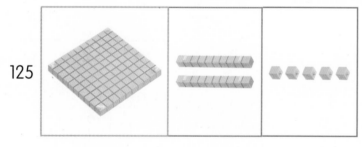

125

So, 249 − 124 = 125.

Check

```
  1 2 5
+ 1 2 4
-------
  2 4 9
```

Work in pairs.

① Subtract 205 from 519.
Show your work.

Hundreds	Tens	Ones
◯	◯	◯
− ◯	◯	◯
◯	◯	◯

② Ask your partner to use [blocks] to check your work.

③ Trade places. Repeat ① and ② by subtracting 52 from 968.

Hundreds	Tens	Ones
◯	◯	◯
− ◯	◯	◯
◯	◯	◯

TRY Practice subtracting within 1,000 without regrouping

Subtract mentally.

① 684 – 4 = _____

② 684 – 40 = _____

③ 684 – 400 = _____

Subtract.

4 175 − 43 = ?

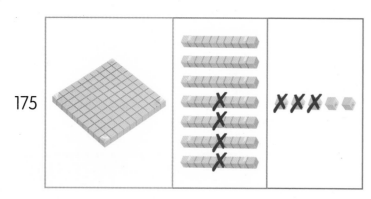

175

$$\begin{array}{r} 1\ 7\ 5 \\ -\quad 4\ 3 \\ \hline \end{array}$$

So, 175 − 43 = _____.

Check

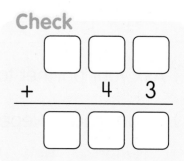

$$\begin{array}{r} \square\ \square\ \square \\ +\qquad 4\ \ 3 \\ \hline \square\ \square\ \square \end{array}$$

5
$$\begin{array}{r} 5\ 7\ 4 \\ -\quad 5\ 3 \\ \hline \end{array}$$

6
$$\begin{array}{r} 6\ 9\ 5 \\ -\ 3\ 6\ 2 \\ \hline \end{array}$$

Subtract.
Show your work.

7 475 − 54 = _____

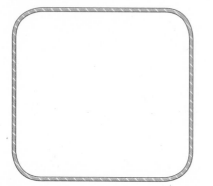

8 783 − 432 = _____

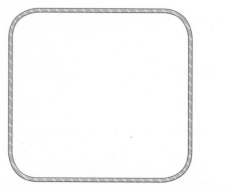

INDEPENDENT PRACTICE

Subtract mentally.

1. 408 – 1 = _____

2. 655 – 40 = _____

3. 726 – 200 = _____

Subtract.

4.
```
   1 6 4
 –   2 3
```

5.
```
   6 8 5
 –   7 1
```

6.
```
   6 9 3
 – 3 4 2
```

7.
```
   7 5 7
 – 5 2 7
```

8.
```
   3 8 5
 – 1 8 4
```

9.
```
   5 7 2
 – 2 6 2
```

10.
```
   8 4 5
 – 4 2 3
```

11.
```
   9 9 9
 – 8 7 6
```

Subtract.
Show your work.

12 797 – 13 = _____

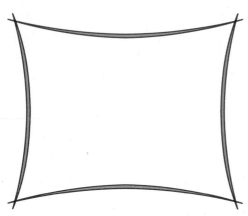

13 864 – 52 = _____

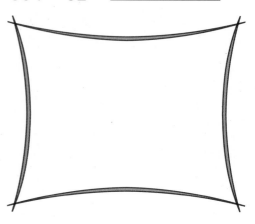

14 685 – 424 = _____

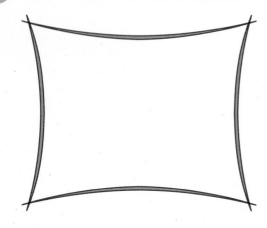

15 476 – 371 = _____

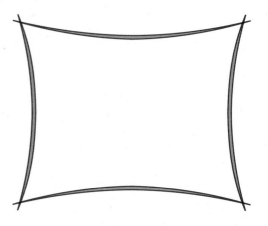

16 245 – 103 = _____

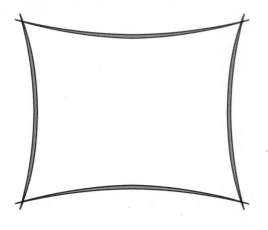

17 586 – 263 = _____

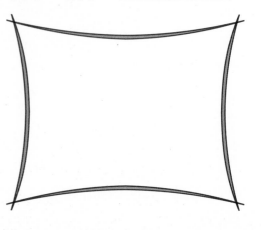

3 Subtracting with Regrouping in Tens and Ones

Learning Objective:
• Use subtraction strategies and algorithm to subtract up to 3-digit numbers with regrouping in tens and ones.

THINK

Find each missing digit.

```
    7  ?  2
 -  ?  6  5
 ----------
    3  2  7
```

Share the steps to find the missing digits with your partner.

ENGAGE

① Use  to show 256.

Regroup the tens and ones, then subtract 18 from 256.

② Find the missing number in the subtraction sentence.

_____ − 17 = 428

LEARN Subtract within 1,000 with regrouping in tens and ones

① Farmer Cruz collected 242 eggs.
Farmer Reyes collected 128 eggs.
How many more eggs did Farmer Cruz collect than Farmer Reyes?
Subtract 128 from 242 to find out.

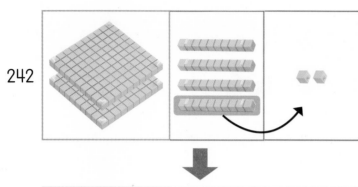

242

Step 1
Regroup the tens and ones.
4 tens 2 ones = 3 tens 12 ones

```
        3   12
    2   4   2
  - 1   2   8
```

Step 2
Subtract the ones.

```
        3   12
    2   4   2
  - 1   2   8
            4
```
12 ones – 8 ones
= 4 ones

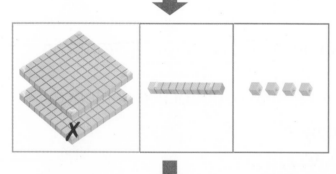

Step 3
Subtract the tens.

```
        3   12
    2   4   2
  - 1   2   8
        1   4
```
3 tens – 2 tens
= 1 ten

Step 4
Subtract the hundreds.

```
        3   12
    2   4   2
  - 1   2   8
    1   1   4
```
2 hundreds
– 1 hundred
= 1 hundred

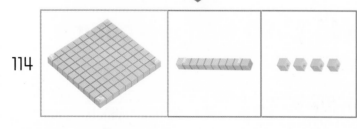

114

So, 242 – 128 = 114.
Farmer Cruz collected 114 more eggs than
Farmer Reyes.

Check

```
        1
    1   1   4
  + 1   2   8
    2   4   2
```

Work in pairs.

(1) Subtract 106 from 623.
Show your work.

Hundreds	Tens	Ones
☐	☐	☐
− ☐	☐	☐
☐	☐	☐

(2) Ask your partner to use ▯ to check your work.

(3) Trade places. Repeat (1) and (2) with these numbers.

a Subtract 319 from 865.

Hundreds	Tens	Ones
☐	☐	☐
− ☐	☐	☐
☐	☐	☐

b Subtract 528 from 937.

Hundreds	Tens	Ones
☐	☐	☐
− ☐	☐	☐
☐	☐	☐

TRY Practice subtracting within 1,000 with regrouping in tens and ones

Subtract.

1 278 − 39 = ?

278

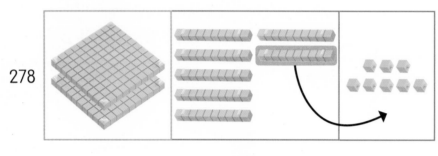

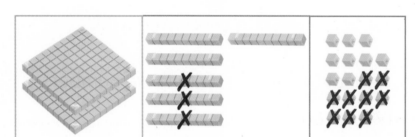

$$\begin{array}{r} 2\ 7\ 8 \\ -\ \ \ 3\ 9 \\ \hline \end{array}$$

So, 278 − 39 = _____.

Check

$$\begin{array}{r} \square\ \square\ \square \\ +\ \ \ 3\ 9 \\ \hline \square\ \square\ \square \end{array}$$

2
$$\begin{array}{r} 2\ 9\ 1 \\ -\ \ \ 5\ 5 \\ \hline \end{array}$$

3
$$\begin{array}{r} 4\ 8\ 5 \\ -\ \ \ 6\ 9 \\ \hline \end{array}$$

4

$$
\begin{array}{r}
6\ 5\ 2 \\
-\quad 2\ 7 \\
\hline
\end{array}
$$

5

$$
\begin{array}{r}
7\ 6\ 3 \\
-\ 2\ 0\ 7 \\
\hline
\end{array}
$$

6

$$
\begin{array}{r}
5\ 4\ 8 \\
-\ 3\ 1\ 9 \\
\hline
\end{array}
$$

7

$$
\begin{array}{r}
9\ 7\ 7 \\
-\ 4\ 6\ 8 \\
\hline
\end{array}
$$

Subtract.
Show your work.

8 173 − 54 = _____

9 365 − 38 = _____

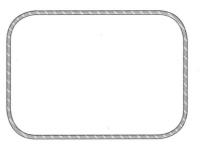

10 594 − 47 = _____

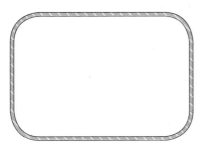

11 281 − 146 = _____

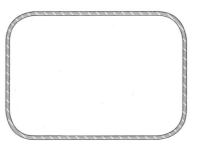

12 735 − 307 = _____

13 847 − 519 = _____

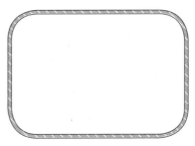

ENGAGE

1 Draw number bonds to find each missing number.

    a   10 – _____ = 9   **b**   10 – _____ = 7

    Complete: Subtracting _____ is the same as subtracting 10

    and adding _____.

2 How can you use the subtraction sentences in **1** to subtract 7 from 113?

LEARN Subtract ones from a 3-digit number mentally

1   164 – 9 = ?

    STEP 1   Subtract 9 from 10.
                10 – 9 = 1

    STEP 2   Add 1 to 154.
                154 + 1 = 155

    So, 164 – 9 = 155.

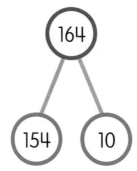

2   545 – 7 = ?

    STEP 1   Subtract 10 from 545.
                545 – 10 = 535

    STEP 2   Add 3 to the result.
                535 + 3 = 538

    So, 545 – 7 = 538.

7 and 3 make 10.

TRY Practice subtracting ones from a 3-digit number mentally

Subtract mentally.

1   372 – 8 = _____   **2**   543 – 6 = _____

3   625 – 9 = _____   **4**   786 – 7 = _____

Name: _____ Date: _____

INDEPENDENT PRACTICE

Subtract.

①
```
    5 3 6
  –   1 8
  ───────
```

②
```
    3 9 2
  –   4 5
  ───────
```

③
```
    7 8 4
  –   7 6
  ───────
```

④
```
    6 6 1
  – 2 4 6
  ───────
```

⑤
```
    8 5 4
  – 3 1 7
  ───────
```

⑥
```
    5 5 5
  – 2 4 6
  ───────
```

Subtract.
Show your work.

⑦ 562 – 47 = _____

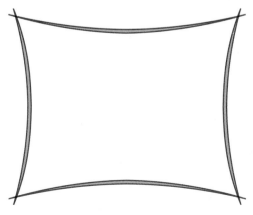

⑧ 397 – 88 = _____

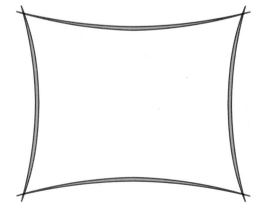

9 785 – 457 = _____

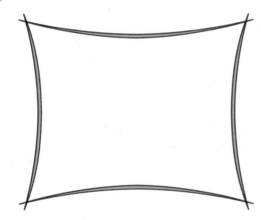

10 553 – 406 = _____

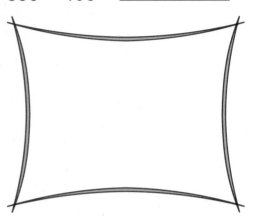

11 641 – 327 = _____

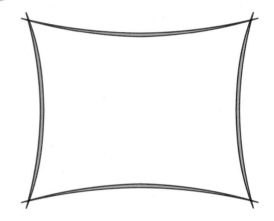

12 978 – 539 = _____

Subtract mentally.

13 231 – 7 = _____

14 586 – 8 = _____

15 493 – 6 = _____

16 728 – 9 = _____

17 654 – 5 = _____

18 842 – 8 = _____

Subtracting with Regrouping in Hundreds and Tens

Learning Objective:
- Use subtraction strategies and algorithm to subtract up to 3-digit numbers with regrouping in hundreds and tens.

THINK

Find each missing digit.

```
    ?   ?   9
  -     5   8   ?
  _____
      3   6   4
```

Share the steps to find the missing digits with your partner.

ENGAGE

1 Use ▧ to show 205.

Regroup the hundreds and tens, then subtract 13 from 205.

2 Find the missing number where its hundreds and tens were regrouped in the subtraction sentence.

_____ − 95 = 523

LEARN Subtract within 1,000 with regrouping in hundreds and tens

1 There were 317 toy cars in a store.
172 toy cars were sold.
How many toy cars were left in the store?
Subract 172 from 317 to find out.

317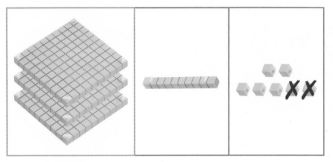

Step 1
Subtract the ones.

	3	1	7
−	1	7	2
			5

7 ones − 2 ones
= 5 ones

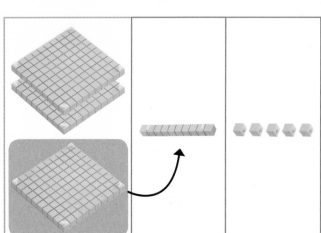

Step 2
Regroup the hundreds and tens.

3 hundreds 1 ten
= 2 hundreds 11 tens

	2	11	
	3̶	1̶	7
−	1	7	2
			5

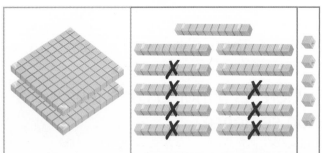

Step 3
Subtract the tens.

	2	11	
	3̶	1̶	7
−	1	7	2
		4	5

11 tens − 7 tens
= 4 tens

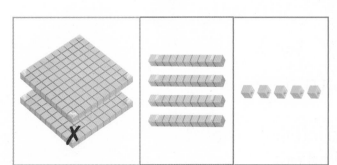

Step 4
Subtract the hundreds.

	2	11	
	3̶	1̶	7
−	1	7	2
	1	4	5

2 hundreds
− 1 hundred
= 1 hundred

145

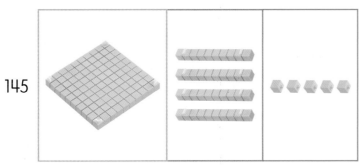

So, 317 − 172 = 145.
145 toy cars were left in the store.

Check

$$\begin{array}{r} {\scriptstyle 1} \\ 1\ 4\ 5 \\ +\ 1\ 7\ 2 \\ \hline 3\ 1\ 7 \end{array}$$

Hands-on Activity Subtracting within 1,000 with regrouping in hundreds and tens

Work in pairs.

(1) Subtract 372 from 568.
Show your work.

Hundreds	Tens	Ones
☐	☐	☐
− ☐	☐	☐
☐	☐	☐

(2) Ask your partner to use ▨ to check your work.

(3) Trade places. Repeat (1) and (2) by subtracting 231 from 726.

Hundreds	Tens	Ones
☐	☐	☐
− ☐	☐	☐
☐	☐	☐

TRY Practice subtracting within 1,000 with regrouping in hundreds and tens

Subtract.

1 217 − 77 = ?

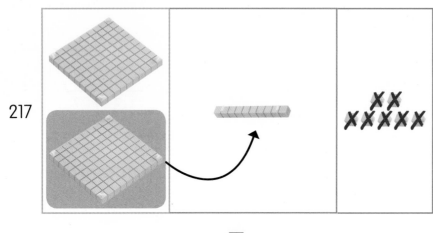

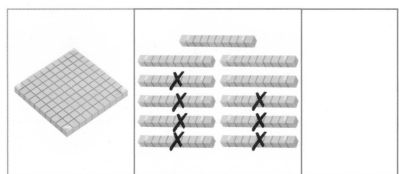

$$\begin{array}{r} 2\ 1\ 7 \\ -\quad 7\ 7 \\ \hline \end{array}$$

So, 217 − 77 = _____ .

Check

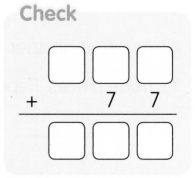

$$\begin{array}{r} \square\ \square\ \square \\ +\quad 7\ 7 \\ \hline \square\ \square\ \square \end{array}$$

2
$$\begin{array}{r} 3\ 1\ 5 \\ -\ 1\ 8\ 2 \\ \hline \end{array}$$

3
$$\begin{array}{r} 7\ 4\ 6 \\ -\ 3\ 5\ 0 \\ \hline \end{array}$$

ENGAGE

1 Draw number bonds to find each missing number.

    a   100 – _____ = 80   **b**   100 – _____ = 60

2 How can you use the subtraction sentences in **1** to subtract 60 from 438?

LEARN Subtract tens from a 3-digit number mentally

1 115 – 70 = ?

    STEP 1 Subtract 70 from 100.
              100 – 70 = 30

    STEP 2 Add 15 to the result.
              30 + 15 = 45

So, 115 – 70 = 45.

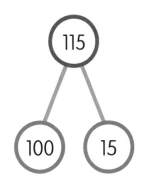

2 529 – 80 = ?

    STEP 1 Subtract 100 from 529.
              529 – 100 = 429

    STEP 2 Add 20 to the result.
              429 + 20 = 449

So, 529 – 80 = 449.

80 and 20 make 100.

TRY Practice subtracting tens from a 3-digit number mentally

Subtract mentally.

1 124 – 60 = _____

2 467 – 80 = _____

3 618 – 90 = _____

4 951 – 70 = _____

BREAK A HUNDRED!

What you need:

Players: 3–4

Materials: one ,

What to do:

1. Player 1 will be the banker.

2. Each player gets 5 ⬙ from the banker.

3. Player 2 rolls the 🎲.
   Player 1 takes away this number of ▭▭▭▭ from Player 2.

4. Players take turns to roll the 🎲.
   Players may trade 1 ◇ for ▭▭▭▭ if they need to.

Who is the winner?

The first player to give away all the ◇ and ▭▭▭▭ wins.

Name: _____ Date: _____

INDEPENDENT PRACTICE

Subtract.

1   2 3 9
     −   6 7

2   5 7 6
     −   8 5

3   3 4 8
     −   9 2

4   6 3 8
     − 3 5 6

5   5 7 8
     − 1 8 0

6   6 5 4
     − 2 9 3

Subtract.
Show your work.

7   456 − 63 = _____

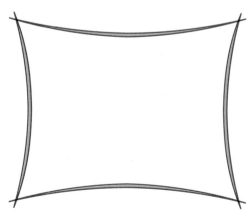

8   729 − 71 = _____

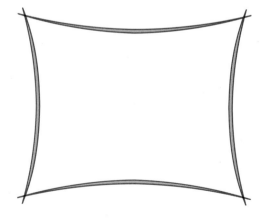

9 439 – 186 = _____

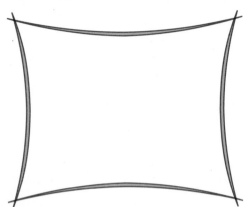

10 828 – 567 = _____

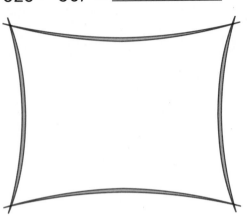

11 648 – 463 = _____

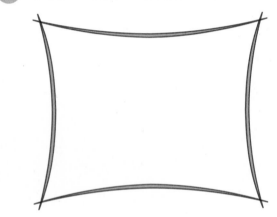

12 964 – 592 = _____

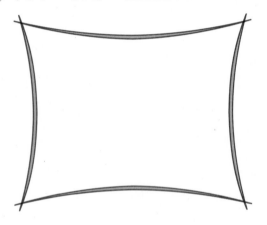

Subtract mentally.

13 346 – 50 = _____

14 521 – 70 = _____

15 675 – 80 = _____

16 769 – 90 = _____

17 837 – 60 = _____

18 918 – 70 = _____

5 Subtracting with Regrouping in Hundreds, Tens, and Ones

Lesson Objective:
• Use subtraction strategies and algorithm to subtract up to 3-digit numbers with regrouping in hundreds, tens, and ones.

THINK

Find each missing digit.

$$
\begin{array}{r}
\boxed{?}\ \boxed{?}\ 3 \\
-\ \ 6\ \ 7\ \ \boxed{?} \\
\hline
1\ \ 7\ \ 4
\end{array}
$$

Share the steps to find the missing digits with your partner.

ENGAGE

Use ▦ to show 312.

Show how you can use ▦ to take away 123.

Now, use ▦ to show 432.

Take away 234.

What do you notice about the regrouping?

LEARN Subtract within 1,000 with regrouping in hundreds, tens, and ones

1. A school bought 432 pens.
   178 were blue pens and the rest were black.
   How many black pens did the school buy?
   Subtract 178 from 432 to find out.

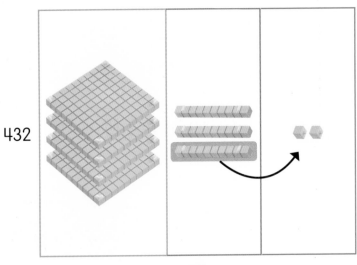

432

Step 1
Regroup the tens
and ones.

3 tens 2 ones
= 2 tens 12 ones

	2	12
4	3̸	2̸
− 1	7	8

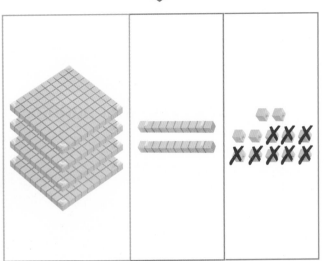

Step 2
Subtract the ones.

	2	12
4	3̸	2̸
− 1	7	8
		4

12 ones − 8 ones
= 4 ones

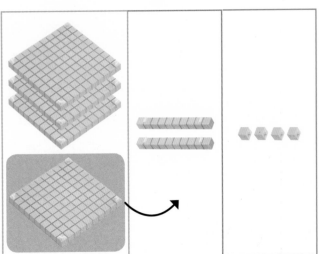

Step 3
Regroup the hundreds
and tens.

4 hundreds 2 tens
= 3 hundreds 12 tens

	3	12	12
4̸	3̸	2̸	
− 1	7	8	
			4

© 2020 Marshall Cavendish Education Pte Ltd

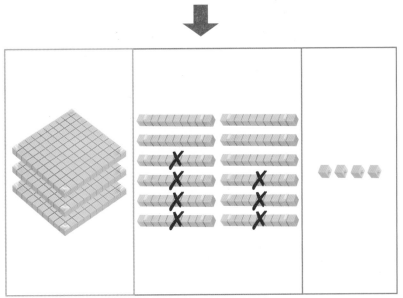

Step 4
Subtract the tens.

	3	12	12
	4	3̶	2̶
−	1	7	8
		5	4

12 tens − 7 tens = 5 tens

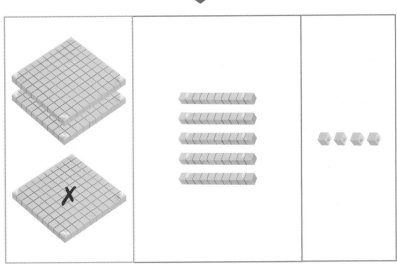

Step 5
Subtract the hundreds.

	3	12	12
	4̶	3̶	2̶
−	1	7	8
	2	5	4

3 hundreds −
1 hundred
= 2 hundreds

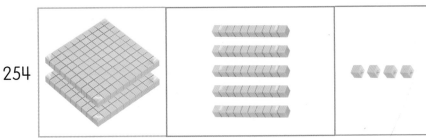

254

So, 432 − 178 = 254.
The school bought 254 black pens.

Check

	1	1	
	2	5	4
+	1	7	8
	4	3	2

Hands-on Activity Subtracting within 1,000 with regrouping
in hundreds, tens, and ones

Work in pairs.

(1) Subtract 168 from 453.
Show your work.

Hundreds	Tens	Ones
☐	☐	☐
− ☐	☐	☐
☐	☐	☐

(2) Ask your partner to use  to check your work.

(3) Trade places. Repeat (1) and (2) by subtracting 572 from 921.

Hundreds	Tens	Ones
☐	☐	☐
− ☐	☐	☐
☐	☐	☐

Math Talk

732 − 248 = 516
Is the answer correct?
Talk to your partner about how you get your answer.

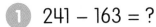 **Practice subtracting within 1,000 with regrouping in hundreds, tens, and ones**

Subtract.

1 241 − 163 = ?

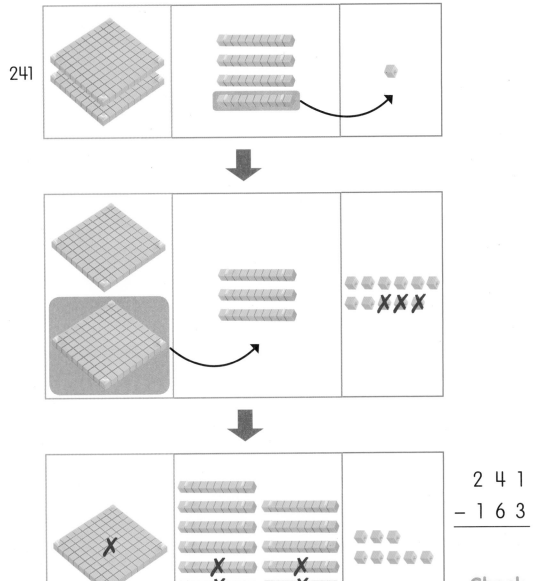

241

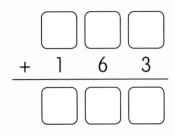

```
   2 4 1
 − 1 6 3
```

Check

```
 +   1   6   3
```

So, 241 − 163 = _____.

②
```
    5 5 5
  −   5 7
  _____
```

③
```
    8 1 6
  −   8 9
  _____
```

④
```
    4 7 8
  − 1 7 9
  _____
```

⑤
```
    6 5 2
  − 4 6 5
  _____
```

⑥
```
    7 3 4
  − 5 7 8
  _____
```

⑦
```
    9 8 7
  − 6 9 8
  _____
```

Subtract.
Show your work.

⑧ 415 − 37 = _____

⑨ 576 − 87 = _____

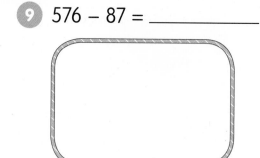

⑩ 324 − 186 = _____

⑪ 861 − 265 = _____

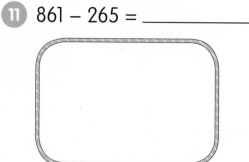

INDEPENDENT PRACTICE

Subtract.

1
```
  3 4 7
-   6 9
-------
```

2
```
  6 2 1
-   5 7
-------
```

3
```
  2 5 8
- 1 7 9
-------
```

4
```
  9 6 2
- 3 8 5
-------
```

5
```
  4 7 3
- 1 8 6
-------
```

6
```
  8 6 2
- 6 7 3
-------
```

7
```
  5 3 5
- 4 6 8
-------
```

8
```
  7 8 4
- 5 8 6
-------
```

9
```
  8 8 3
- 1 9 5
-------
```

10
```
  4 4 6
- 2 7 8
-------
```

Subtract.
Show your work.

11 827 − 59 = _____

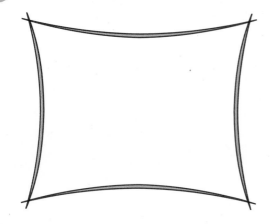

12 615 − 78 = _____

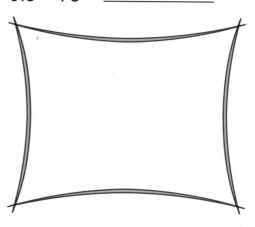

13 382 − 194 = _____

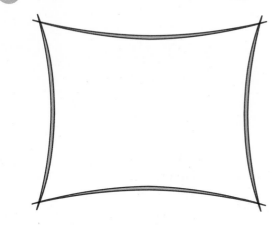

14 753 − 594 = _____

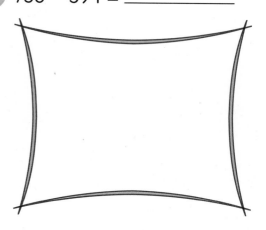

15 934 − 468 = _____

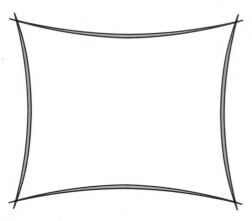

16 543 − 259 = _____

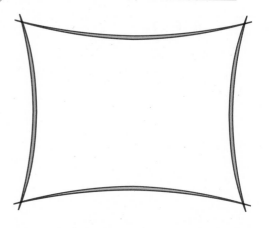

Subtracting Across Zeros

Learning Objective:
• Subtract from 3-digit numbers with zeros by regrouping in hundreds, tens, and ones.

 **THINK**

Find each missing digit.

```
    7   0   0
 - [?]  7  [?]
 ───────────────
    5   2   8
```

Share the steps to find the missing digits with your partner.

ENGAGE

Taylor spent $72 on a dress.
She paid the cashier with a $100 note.
How much change did she receive?
Explore two ways to find the answer with your partner.

LEARN Subtract from numbers with zeros

1. There were 200 paper clips in a box.
   Madelyn used 18 paper clips.
   How many paper clips were left in the box?
   Subract 18 from 200 to find out.

200

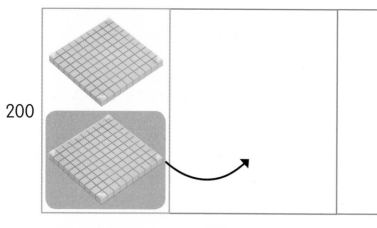

Step 1
Regroup the hundreds and tens.

2 hundreds
= 1 hundred 10 tens

	$\overset{1}{\cancel{2}}$	$\overset{10}{\cancel{0}}$	0
−		1	8

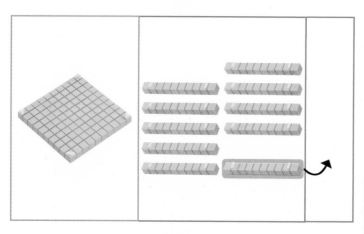

Step 2
Regroup the tens and ones.

10 tens
= 9 tens 10 ones

	$\overset{1}{\cancel{2}}$	$\overset{9}{\cancel{\cancel{0}}}$	$\overset{10}{\cancel{0}}$
−		1	8

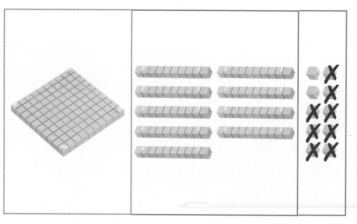

Step 3
Subtract the ones.

	$\overset{1}{\cancel{2}}$	$\overset{9}{\cancel{\cancel{0}}}$	$\overset{10}{\cancel{0}}$
−		1	8
			2

10 ones − 8 ones
= 2 ones

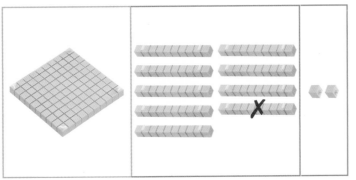

Step 4
Subtract the tens.

$$
\begin{array}{r}
\overset{1}{\cancel{2}}\ \overset{9}{\cancel{\underset{10}{10}}\cancel{0}}\ \cancel{0} \\
-\quad 1\ 8 \\
\hline
8\ 2
\end{array}
$$

9 tens − 1 ten
= 8 tens

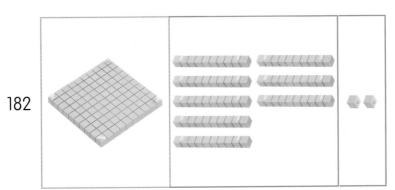

182

Step 5
Subtract the hundreds.

$$
\begin{array}{r}
\overset{1}{\cancel{2}}\ \overset{9}{\cancel{\underset{10}{10}}\cancel{0}}\ \cancel{0} \\
-\quad 1\ 8 \\
\hline
1\ 8\ 2
\end{array}
$$

1 hundred
− 0 hundreds
= 1 hundred

Check

$$
\begin{array}{r}
\overset{1}{\ }\ \overset{1}{\ } \\
1\ 8\ 2 \\
+\quad 1\ 8 \\
\hline
2\ 0\ 0
\end{array}
$$

So, 200 − 18 = 182.
182 paper clips were left in the box.

 **Math Talk**

Your partner subtracts 157 from 400 as shown.

$$
\begin{array}{r}
4\ 0\ 0 \\
-\ 1\ 5\ 7 \\
\hline
3\ 5\ 7
\end{array}
$$

Do you know why your partner did this?
Show and tell your partner the correct way to subtract.

TRY Practice subtracting from numbers with zeros

Subtract.

1. 300 – 87 = ?

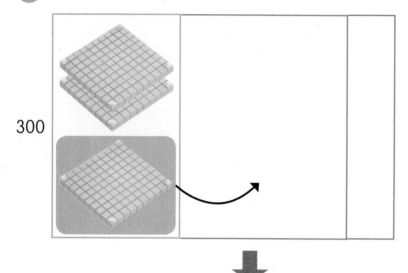

300

Regroup the hundreds, tens, and ones in 300.
300 = 3 hundreds
    = 2 hundreds
      9 tens 10 ones

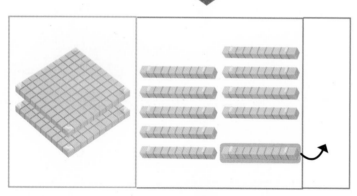

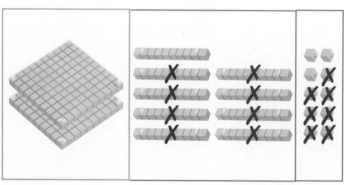

$$\begin{array}{r} 3\ 0\ 0 \\ -\ \ \ 8\ 7 \\ \hline \end{array}$$

Check

So, 300 – 87 = _____.

②
```
   1 0 0
 -   9 8
 _____
```

③
```
   7 0 0
 -   2 9
 _____
```

④
```
   5 0 0
 - 2 6 7
 _____
```

⑤
```
   6 0 0
 - 3 0 5
 _____
```

⑥
```
   8 0 0
 - 2 4 4
 _____
```

⑦
```
   9 0 0
 - 1 5 1
 _____
```

Mathematical Habit 7 **Make use of structure**

Look at the mathematical sentence.
How can you find the missing number?

$$? + 4 = 20 - 5$$

Which part of the sentence can you solve first?

20 − 5 = 15
So, ? + 4 = 15

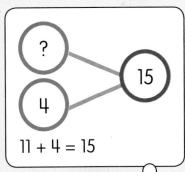

11 + 4 = 15

The missing number is 11.
Use the method shown to find the missing number in
37 + 10 + 10 = ? + 12.

4 IN A ROW!

What you need:

Players: 2–4
Materials: Number grid, Subtraction number cards,

What to do:

1. Player 1 takes a card and subtracts the numbers on it.

2. The other players check that Player 1's answer is correct.

3. If Player 1's answer is on the number grid, place a counter on that number.

314	495	463	371
148	239	551	362
376	284	161	359
249	489	472	393

If player 1's answer is incorrect, a counter will not be placed on the number grid.

4. Take turns to play.
Do not return the cards to the deck after each turn.

Who is the winner?

The first player to get 4 counters in a row wins.

INDEPENDENT PRACTICE
Subtract.

1)
```
   2 0 0
 –   4 5
 ───────
```

2)
```
   4 0 0
 –   9 9
 ───────
```

3)
```
   7 0 0
 – 2 8 8
 ───────
```

4)
```
   9 0 0
 – 6 9 8
 ───────
```

5)
```
   8 0 0
 – 4 5 6
 ───────
```

6)
```
   5 0 0
 – 3 7 2
 ───────
```

7)
```
   3 0 0
 – 1 8 3
 ───────
```

8)
```
   6 0 0
 – 3 1 7
 ───────
```

9)
```
   4 0 0
 – 2 6 1
 ───────
```

10)
```
   9 0 0
 – 5 2 4
 ───────
```

Subtract.
Show your work.

11   300 − 195 = _____

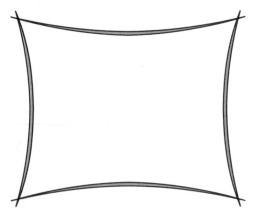

12   600 − 472 = _____

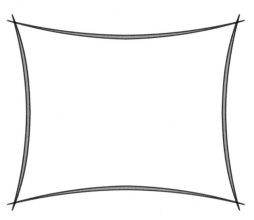

13   900 − 238 = _____

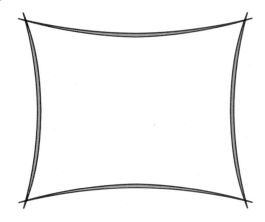

14   400 − 126 = _____

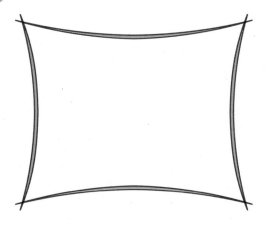

15   700 − 583 = _____

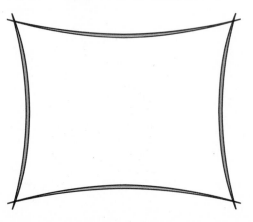

16   500 − 319 = _____

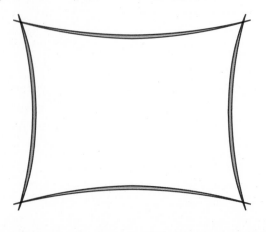

Mathematical Habit 3 Construct viable arguments

The answer in the example is incorrect.
Spot the mistake.
Then, write the correct working.

```
   9 4 4
-  5 6 9
---------
   4 2 5
```

Problem Solving with Heuristics

1 **Mathematical Habit** **1** **Persevere in solving problems**

Make two 3-digit numbers from the numbers below.
Use each number once.
What are the two 3-digit numbers that give the greatest answer
when you subtract them?

3   5   2   4   1   0

Which two digits can
you subtract to get the
greatest hundreds?

2 **Mathematical Habit** **1** **Persevere in solving problems**

Find each missing digit.

a

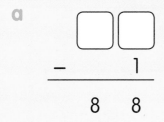

```
   □ □
 −   1
 ───
   8 8
```

b

```
 □ □ □
 − 4 4 4
 ───────
   4 4 4
```

c

```
   6 5 4
 − 2 □ 4
 ───────
   4 2 0
```

What are the ways that you can use to find the missing digits?

CHAPTER WRAP-UP

? What are the ways that you can subtract numbers within 1,000?

Subtraction Within 1,000

Subtracting Mentally

a counting back

17 – 2 = 15

15	16	**17**

b using related addition fact

7 + 5 = 12

12 – 7 = 5

c 569 – 80 = ?

STEP 1 Use 500 to subtract 80.

500 – 80
= 420

STEP 2 Add 69 to the result.

420 + 69 = 489

d 914 – 60 = ?

STEP 1 Subtract 100 from 914.

914 – 100
= 814

STEP 2 Add 40 to the result.

814 + 40
= 854

Subtracting 3-Digit Numbers

a subtract without regrouping

Step 1 Subtract the ones.

Step 2 Subtract the tens.

Step 3 Subtract the hundreds.

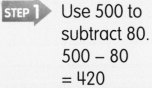

b subtract with regrouping

Step 1 Regroup tens and ones.

Step 2 Subtract the ones.

Step 3 Regroup hundreds and tens.

Step 4 Subtract the tens.

Step 5 Subtract the hundreds.

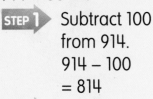

Subtracting with Zeros

Step 1 Regroup hundreds and tens.

Step 2 Regroup tens and ones.

Step 3 Subtract the ones.

Step 4 Subtract the tens.

Step 5 Subtract the hundreds.

```
      9
  4  10  10
   5   0   0
 - 1   9   3
   3   0   7
```

Name: _____   Date: _____

Subtract mentally.

1 15 – 3 = _____

2 12 – 9 = _____

3 76 – 4 = _____

4 98 – 20 = _____

Subtract.

5
```
    8 5
  – 6 7
  _____
```

6
```
    4 2 6
  – 2 3 9
  _____
```

Subtract.
Show your work.

7 897 – 246 = _____

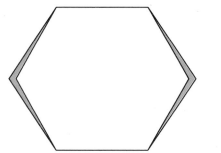

8 356 – 149 = _____

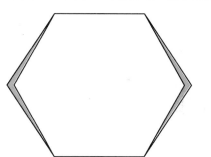

9 677 – 383 = _____

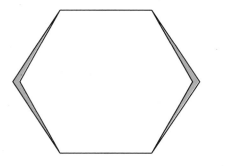

10 400 – 273 = _____

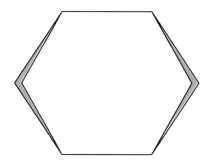

Subtract mentally.

11 718 – 400 = _____

12 463 – 7 = _____

13 254 – 90 = _____

14 549 – 60 = _____

Assessment Prep

Answer each question.

15 Which of the following gives the answer 234?
Make a ✓ in the correct circle.

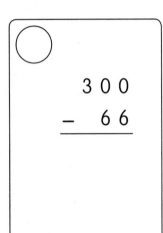

$$\begin{array}{r} 3\,0\,0 \\ -\quad 6\,6 \\ \hline \end{array}$$

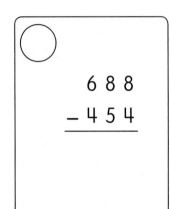

$$\begin{array}{r} 6\,8\,8 \\ -4\,5\,4 \\ \hline \end{array}$$

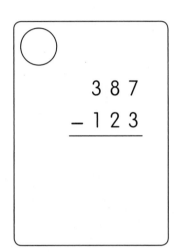

$$\begin{array}{r} 3\,8\,7 \\ -1\,2\,3 \\ \hline \end{array}$$

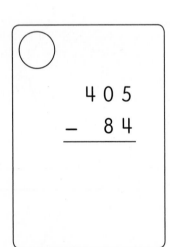

$$\begin{array}{r} 4\,0\,5 \\ -\quad 8\,4 \\ \hline \end{array}$$

$$\begin{array}{r} 4\,6\,7 \\ -2\,3\,3 \\ \hline \end{array}$$

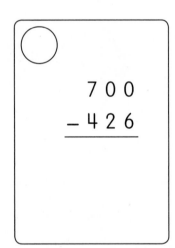

$$\begin{array}{r} 7\,0\,0 \\ -4\,2\,6 \\ \hline \end{array}$$

16 Find the missing digit.

$$\begin{array}{r} 5\ \boxed{}\ 2 \\ -\ 2\ \ 5\ \ 3 \\ \hline 2\ \ 5\ \ 9 \end{array}$$

In a Garden

1 Write the missing digit.

```
      2   5   ☐
  −   1   2   6
  ─────────────
      1   2   4
```

How did you get your answer?
Write down the steps.

2 There are 312 leaves on the grass.
185 leaves are swept away.
How many leaves are there left on the grass?
Show your work.

312 − 185 = _____

There are _____ leaves left on the grass.

3 Find the missing number.
? + 67 = 757

Show your work.

757 − 67 = _____

4 There are 186 insects in a garden.
There are 95 red ants.
There are 64 black ants.
The rest are butterflies.

a How many black ants and butterflies are there?
Show your work.

186 − 95 = _____

There are _____ black ants and butterflies.

b How many butterflies are there?
Show your work.

_____ − 64 = _____

There are _____ butterflies.

Rubric

Point(s)	Level	My Performance
7–8	4	• Most of my answers are correct. • I show all my work correctly. • I explain my thinking clearly and completely.
5–6.5	3	• Some of my answers are correct. • I show some of my work correctly. • I explain my thinking clearly.
3–4.5	2	• A few of my answers are correct. • I show little work correctly. • I explain some of my thinking clearly.
0–2.5	1	• A few of my answers are correct. • I show little or no work. • I do not explain my thinking clearly.

Teacher's Comments

Chapter 4
Using Bar Models: Addition and Subtraction

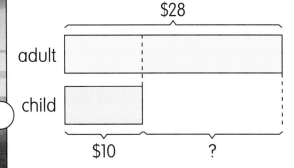

How much more does a meal for an adult cost than a meal for a child on a weekday?

$28

adult

child

$10   ?

$28 − $10 = $18

Dinner Special

Weekday
Adult $28
Child $10

Weekend
Adult $32
Child $14

When do you use addition and subtraction in real-world problems?

Name: _____ Date: _____

Adding and subtracting without regrouping

a
```
    2  3  5
 +  3  2  4
 ─────────
    5  5  9
```

b
```
    5  7  9
 −  2  4  5
 ─────────
    3  3  4
```

▶ Quick Check

Add or subtract.

①
```
    4  5  7
 +  5  4  1
 ─────────
```

②
```
    7  3  9
 −  6  1  8
 ─────────
```

Adding and subtracting with regrouping

a
```
    1  1
    3  2  6
 +  1  8  5
 ─────────
    5  1  1
```

b
```
    7  11 15
    8̶  2̶  5̶
 −  3  6  7
 ─────────
    4  5  8
```

▶ Quick Check

Add or subtract.

③
```
    2  6  8
 +  5  9  7
 ─────────
```

④
```
    5  0  0
 −  2  2  5
 ─────────
```

Solving real-world problems involving addition and subtraction

a   A farmer has 12 chicks and 8 hens.
How many chicks and hens does she have in all?

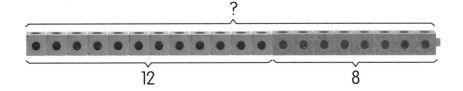

12 + 8 = 20

She has 20 chicks and hens in all.

b   A teacher has 25 pens and pencils in all.
He has 15 pens.
How many pencils does he have?

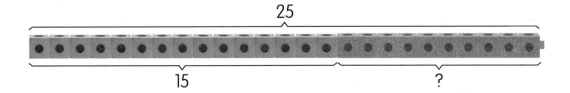

25 − 15 = 10

He has 10 pencils.

c Logan has 16 pennies in his coin box.
His sister has 7 fewer pennies than him.
How many pennies does his sister have?

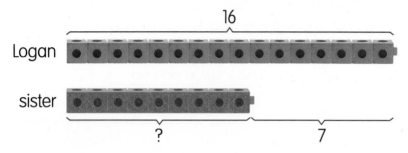

16 − 7 = 9

His sister has 9 pennies.

d Mr. Moore bakes 6 chocolate muffins, 5 banana muffins, and
4 blueberry muffins.
How many muffins does he bake in all?

6 + 5 = 11

11 + 4 = 15

He bakes 15 muffins in all.

▶ **Quick Check**

Solve.

Use to help you.

⑤ Mason has 5 blue stickers.
He has 7 yellow stickers.
How many stickers does he have in all?

_____ ◯ _____ = _____

He has _____ stickers in all.

⑥ There are 25 people in a tour group.
There are 16 adults and the rest are children.
How many children are there?

_____ ◯ _____ = _____

There are _____ children.

7 Ellie has 16 medals.
Henry has 5 more medals than Ellie.
How many medals does Henry have?

Henry has _____ medals.

8 Ms. Smith has 8 red balloons, 7 blue balloons,
and 2 white balloons.
How many balloons does she have in all?

She has _____ balloons in all.

Using Part-Whole in Addition and Subtraction

Learning Objective:
• Use bar models to interpret and represent the part-whole concept in addition and subtraction.

> **New Vocabulary**
> bar model

THINK

Naomi has some coins in three cups.
The first cup contains 6 coins.
The second cup contains more coins than the third cup.
The first cup has the most number of coins.

a   What is the least possible number of coins Naomi has?

b   What is the greatest possible number of coins Naomi has?

ENGAGE

1   Solve this problem using  .
There are 7 apples and 9 oranges in a box.
How many apples and oranges are there in all?

2   Take fewer than 20 🎲 and 🎲.
Use the 🎲🎲 to tell an addition story to your partner.
Draw a bar model with your partner to represent the problem.

LEARN Add sets of objects

1 Molly has 8 yellow cubes.
Lucy has 7 red cubes.
How many cubes do they have in all?

STEP 1 Understand the problem.

> How many cubes does Molly have?
> How many cubes does Lucy have?
> What do I need to find?

STEP 2 Think of a plan.
First, I can use 🎲 to show the problem.
Then, I can draw a bar model to show the parts and the whole.

STEP 3 Carry out the plan.

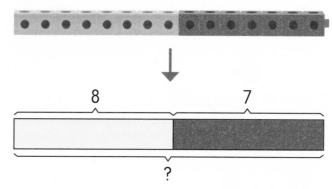

$8 + 7 = 15$
They have 15 cubes in all.

STEP 4 Check the answer.
I can work backwards from the answer.

> $15 - 7 = 8$
> My answer is correct.

① Read the problem.

Julia has 15 strawberries.
Adam has 32 strawberries.
How many strawberries do they have in all?

② Write what you understand and what you need to find.
I understand

a _____

b _____

I need to find _____

③ **Mathematical Habit 4** **Use mathematical models**

Draw a bar model to show the problem.

④ Complete the addition sentence.

_____ + _____ = _____

⑤ Use subtraction to check your answer.

_____ − _____ = _____

⑥ Repeat ② to ⑤ for the following problem.

Store A sells 172 apples.
Store B sells 56 apples.
How many apples do both stores sell in all?
I understand

a _____

b _____

I need to find _____

_____ + _____ = _____

Check: _____ – _____ = _____

TRY Practice adding sets of objects

Solve.
Use the bar model to help you.

1 A restaurant bought 72 bags of potatoes last week.
The same restaurant bought 28 bags
of potatoes this week.
How many bags of potatoes did
the restaurant buy in all?

Use the four-step problem-
solving model to help you.

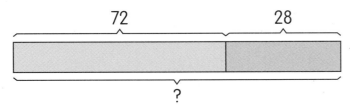

```
72              28
```

?

_____ ◯ _____ = _____

The restaurant bought _____
bags of potatoes in all.

Check

_____ – _____ = _____

_____ – _____ = _____

Is the answer correct?

2 A library has 256 English books.
The librarian buys 184 Spanish books.
How many English and Spanish books are there in all?

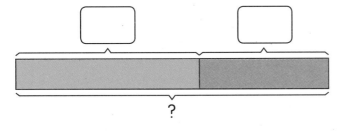

?

_____ ◯ _____ = _____

There are _____ English and
Spanish books in all.

Check

_____ – _____ = _____

_____ – _____ = _____

Is the answer correct?

3 There are 153 adults and 32 children at a party.
How many people are there at the party?

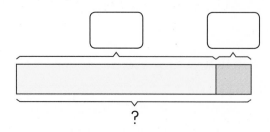

_____ ◯ _____ = _____

There are _____ people at the party.

4 Mr. Kim collects 193 key chains.
Ms. Wood collects 476 key chains.
How many key chains do they collect in all?

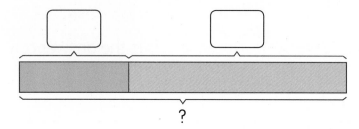

_____ ◯ _____ = _____

They collect _____ key chains in all.

3 There are 303 people at a park.
78 of them are children and the rest are adults.
How many adults are there at the park?

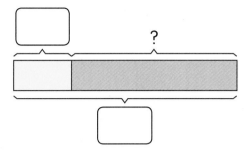

_____ ◯ _____ = _____

There are _____ adults at the park.

4 A library has 648 books.
152 books are loaned out.
How many books are left?

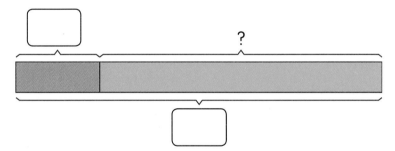

_____ ◯ _____ = _____

_____ books are left.

WRITE AND SOLVE!

What you need:

Players: 2

Materials: , Number cards

What to do:

1. Place the stack of number cards on your desk.

2. Pick two number cards from the stack.

3. Use the numbers on the cards to write an addition or subtraction problem.

   Use to make a model to solve the real-world problem.

4. Check your partner's answer.

5. Your partner receives two points for a correct problem and answer.

6. Trade places. Repeat 2 to 5.

Example
Kiri has 11 teddy bears.
3 of them are big.
The rest are small.
How many teddy bears are small?

Who is the winner?

The player with more points after five rounds wins.

INDEPENDENT PRACTICE

Solve.
Use the bar model to help you.

1 There are 32 boys and 27 girls at a concert.
How many children are there at the concert?

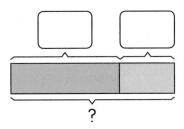

2 A restaurant sells 105 breakfasts in the morning.
It sells 99 lunches in the afternoon.
How many breakfasts and lunches does the restaurant sell in all?

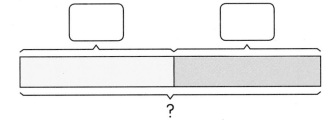

Solve.
Draw a bar model to help you.

3 Ravi has 545 badges.
His sister has 249 badges.
How many badges do they have in all?

4 A store sold 437 books.
There were 352 books left.
How many books were there in the store at first?

5 Chris made 65 clay pots in two weeks.
He made 23 clay pots in Week 1 and the rest in Week 2.
How many clay pots did he make in Week 2?

6 A factory made 425 dolls in two months.
77 dolls were made in June and the rest in July.
How many dolls did the factory make in July?

7 There are 278 people at a parade.
126 of them are adults and the rest are children.
How many children are there?

8 A toy store owner has 999 toys.
He sells 306 toys.
How many toys are left?

 Adding On and Taking Away Sets

Learning Objective:
- Use bar models to interpret and represent the adding-on concept in addition and the taking-away concept in subtraction.

THINK

Aki has 73 bicycles in his store.
He buys some more bicycles.
The number of bicycles he has now is greater than 95 but less than 100.
What is a possible number of bicycles that Aki buys?

ENGAGE

1. Samuel has 26 stamps.
   His mother gives him 43 more stamps.
   How many stamps does Samuel have in all?

   Complete the bar model below.

   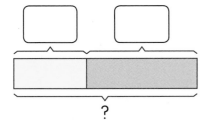

2. Share a similar story with your partner using these words.
   Thomas, Malik, 18, 36, coins, total, gives, at the end

LEARN Add sets of objects

① Lilian has 9 pins.
Jayla gives her 8 more pins.
How many pins does Lilian have now?

STEP 1 Understand the problem.

> How many pins does Lilian have?
> How many pins does Jayla give her?
> What do I need to find?

STEP 2 Think of a plan.
First, I can use ▪▪▪ to show the problem.
Then, I can draw a bar model to show the parts and the whole.

STEP 3 Carry out the plan.

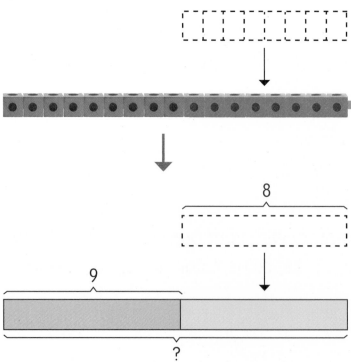

$9 + 8 = 17$

Lilian has 17 pins now.

STEP 4 Check the answer.
I can work backwards.

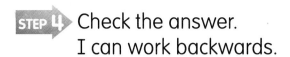

17 − 9 = 8
17 − 8 = 9
My answer is correct.

2 Hana has 9 granola bars.
Her cousin gives her 3 granola bars.
Her brother gives her another 6 granola bars.
How many granola bars does Hana have in all?

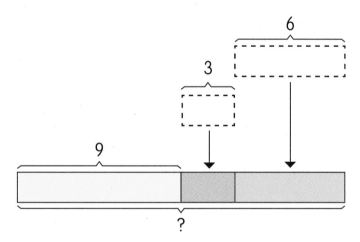

9 + 3 + 6 = 18

Hana has 18 granola bars in all.

Check

18 − 6 = 12
12 − 3 = 9
The answer is correct.

Hands-on Activity Adding sets of objects

1 Read the problem.

Bianca has 34 picture cards.
She then buys 53 more picture cards.
How many picture cards does she have now?

(2) Write what you understand and what you need to find.

I understand

a _____

b _____

I need to find _____

(3) **Mathematical Habit 4** **Use mathematical models**

Draw a bar model to show the problem.

(4) Complete the addition sentence.

_____ + _____ = _____

(5) Use subtraction to check your answer.

_____ – _____ = _____

TRY Practice adding sets of objects

Solve.
Use the bar model to help you.

1. Robert has 24 paper clips.
    His mother gives him 10 paper clips.
    His brother gives him 12 paper clips.
    How many paper clips does he have in all?

Use the four-step problem-solving model to help you.

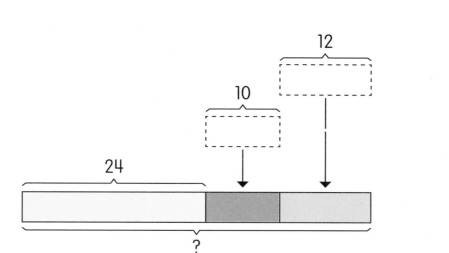

He has _____ paper clips in all.

Check

____ – ____ = ____

____ – ____ = ____

Is the answer correct?

2 A collector has 286 paintings.
She buys 301 more paintings.
How many paintings does she have now?

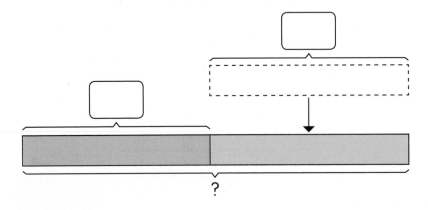

_____ ◯ _____ = _____

She has _____ paintings now.

Check

____ – ____ = ____

____ – ____ = ____

Is the answer correct?

ENGAGE

1 There are 32 students in Mr. Hall's classroom.
15 of the students go to the library.
How many students are left in the classroom?
Draw a bar model to show your thinking.
Share your bar model with your partner.

2 Share a similar story with your partner using these words.
Luis, burgers, 72, 48, in the morning, sold, at the end of the day

LEARN Take away sets to subtract

1 A florist had 98 flowers.
She sold some flowers and had 28 flowers left.
How many flowers did she sell?

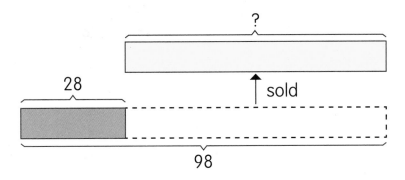

$98 - 28 = 70$

She sold 70 flowers.

Check

$70 + 28 = 98$
The answer is correct.

Read the problem.

A farmer has 120 chickens.
He gives 30 chickens to his brother.
He gives 28 chickens to his sister.
How many chickens does he have left?

How do you draw the bar model for this problem?
Discuss with your partner.

Hands-on Activity ⟩ Making one-step real-world problems

Work in pairs.

① Use the numbers and words in the box to complete this story.

left	gave	412	18	394

Hunter had _____ coins.

He _____ his sister _____ coins.

Hunter had _____ coins _____.

② Repeat ① for these stories.

a

120	buys	more	208	now

Faith has _____ beads.

She _____ 88 _____ beads.

Faith has _____ beads _____.

b

James	31	in all	321	gives	290

_____ has _____ bookmarks.

Alexis _____ him _____ bookmarks.

James has _____ bookmarks _____.

c

_____ has _____ pears in her store.

She _____ 150 _____ .

She has _____ pears _____.

③ Use the words and numbers in the box to write a real-world problem.

gives	32	lemons	46
Olivia	101	78	23
55	Colton	sells	erasers

④ Ask your partner to draw a bar model for the real-world problem. Then, solve.

TRY Practice taking away sets to subtract

Solve.
Use the bar model to help you.

1 Ms. Jones has 40 erasers in her store.
She sells 12 erasers.
How many erasers does she have left?

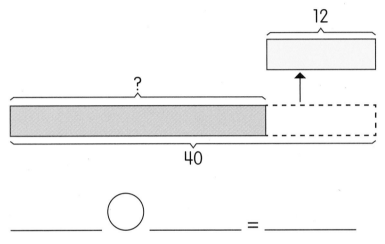

_____ ◯ _____ = _____

She has _____ erasers left.

Check

____ + ____ = ____

Is the answer correct?

2 There are 625 children in the cafeteria.
156 children leave the cafeteria.
How many children are in the cafeteria now?

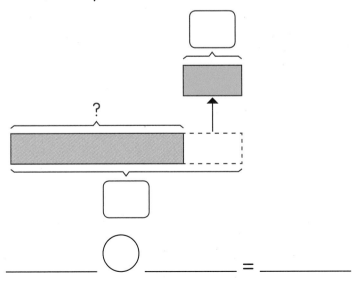

_____ ◯ _____ = _____

There are _____ children in the cafeteria now.

Check

____ + ____ = ____

Is the answer correct?

3 Audrey has 147 toy animals.
She gives her friend 48 toy animals.
How many toy animals does she have left?

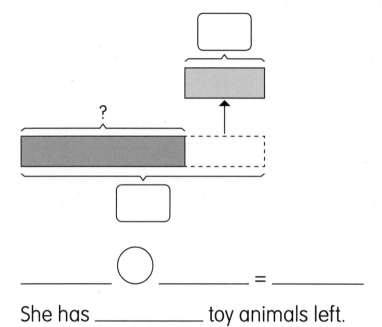

_____ ◯ _____ = _____

She has _____ toy animals left.

4 Mr. Watson has 700 flowers in his store.
He has 258 tulips and the rest are lilies.
How many lilies does he have?

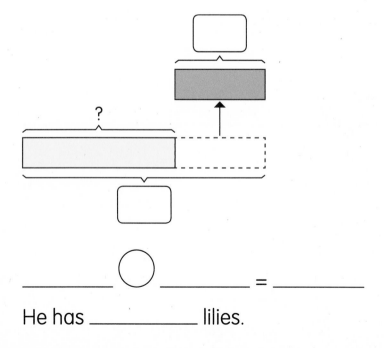

_____ ◯ _____ = _____

He has _____ lilies.

INDEPENDENT PRACTICE

Solve.
Use the bar model to help you.

1 Axel has 54 toy cars.
His sister gives him 36 toy cars.
How many toy cars does he have in all?

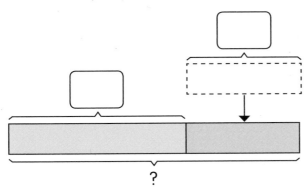

2 Mr. Harris had 99 skateboards in his store.
He sold some skateboards and had 45 skateboards left.
How many skateboards did he sell?

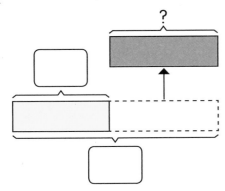

Solve.
Draw a bar model to help you.

3 Ian collected 228 wooden sticks for his art project.
He needed 350 more wooden sticks.
How many wooden sticks did he need for his art project in all?

4 There were 367 bicycles at a rental shop.
174 bicycles were rented out.
How many bicycles were left?

5 Jocelyn walked 95 steps.
She has to walk another 105 steps to reach her school.
How many steps does she have to walk in all?

6 There were 282 people in a hall.
99 people left early.
How many people were left in the hall?

7 A farmer picked 405 mangoes.
   She sold 278 mangoes.
   How many mangoes did she have left?

8 Brayden has 49 magnets.
   His mother gives him 66 magnets.
   His father gives him 34 magnets.
   How many magnets does Brayden have in all?

 Comparing Two Sets

Learning Objective:
• Use bar models to interpret and represent the comparing concept in addition and subtraction.

New Vocabulary
comparison

THINK

A farm has 56 horses and sheep in all.
There are 8 fewer sheep than horses.
How many horses are there on the farm?

ENGAGE

Use fewer than 20 🔲 to make a number train.

Ask your classmate to make a train that is 5 🔲 longer than your train.

Ask another classmate to make a train that is 8 🔲 longer than your train.

Draw three bar models to represent the three trains.

Share how you find the number of 🔲 used to make the trains.

LEARN Compare sets to add

1 Malia has 24 ribbons.
Andrea has 12 more ribbons than Malia.
How many ribbons does Andrea have?

STEP 1 Understand the problem.

How many ribbons does Malia have?
How many more ribbons does Andrea have?
What do I need to find?

STEP 2 Think of a plan.
I can draw a bar model to show the parts and the whole.

STEP 3 Carry out the plan.

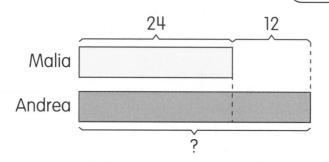

This is a comparison model.

$24 + 12 = 36$

Andrea has 36 ribbons.

$36 - 12 = 24$
My answer is correct.

STEP 4 Check the answer.
I can work backwards.

Hands-on Activity Drawing comparison models

Work in pairs.

Mathematical Habit 4 Use mathematical models

Draw a bar model to show this problem.
Then, solve.

Ricardo has 28 trading cards.
He has 16 fewer trading cards than Aisha.
How many trading cards does Aisha have?

© 2020 Marshall Cavendish Education Pte Ltd

Math Talk

Is it true that you add when you see the words "fewer than"?
Talk to your partner about it.

TRY Practice comparing sets to add

Solve.
Use the bar model to help you.

1   Farmer Wilson has 65 geese on his farm.
Farmer Allen has 18 more geese than Farmer Wilson.
How many geese does Farmer Allen have?

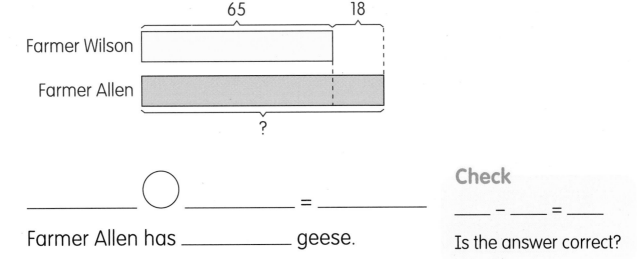

_____ ◯ _____ = _____

Farmer Allen has _____ geese.

Check

_____ – _____ = _____

Is the answer correct?

2 672 people visited the museum on Saturday.
285 more people visited the museum on Sunday than on Saturday.
How many people visited the museum on Sunday?

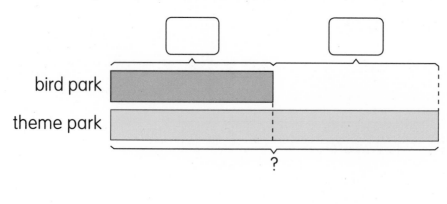

Saturday
Sunday

?

_____ ◯ _____ = _____

_____ people visited the museum on Sunday.

3 305 children went to the bird park.
278 fewer children went to the bird park than to the theme park.
How many children went to the theme park?

bird park
theme park

?

_____ ◯ _____ = _____

_____ children went to the theme park.

ENGAGE

Use fewer than 20 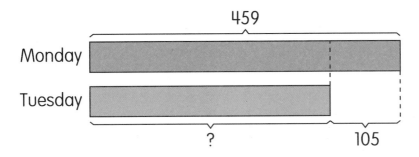 to make a number train.

Make a second train that is shorter than the first.

Make a third train shorter than the second.

Draw three bar models to represent the three trains.

How many fewer are there in the third train than in the first and second trains?

LEARN Compare sets to subtract

1. 459 children were at a carnival on Monday.
   There were 105 fewer children at the carnival on Tuesday.
   How many children were at the carnival on Tuesday?

459 − 105 = 354

354 children were at the carnival on Tuesday.

Check

354 + 105 = 459
The answer is correct.

Hands-on Activity Drawing comparison models

Work in pairs.

Mathematical Habit 4 Use mathematical models

Draw a bar model to show this problem.
Then, solve.

Trevon has 68 toy animals.
He has 16 more toy animals than Morgan.
How many toy animals does Morgan have?

 **Math Talk**

Is it true that you subtract when you see the words "more than"?
Talk to your partner about it.

TRY Practice comparing sets to subtract

Solve.
Use the bar model to help you.

1 Mr. Turner sold 283 T-shirts.
He sold 47 more T-shirts than Ms. Peterson.
How many T-shirts did Ms. Peterson sell?

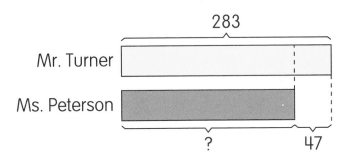

_____ ◯ _____ = _____

Ms. Peterson sold _____ T-shirts.

Check

____ + ____ = ____

Is the answer correct?

2 300 video games are sold in Store A.
126 more video games are sold in Store A than Store B.
How many video games are sold in Store B?

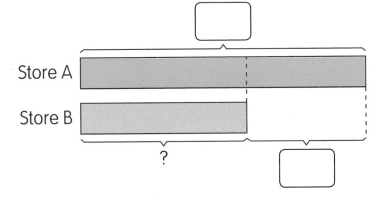

_____ ◯ _____ = _____

_____ video games are sold in Store B.

Check

____ + ____ = ____

Is the answer correct?

3 Bakery A bakes 540 loaves of bread.
Bakery B bakes 210 fewer loaves of bread than Bakery A.
How many loaves of bread does Bakery B bake?

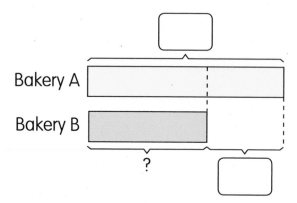

_____ ◯ _____ = _____

Bakery B bakes _____ loaves of bread.

4 Sarah scores 824 points after playing five rounds of bowling.
Miguel scores 157 fewer points than Sarah.
How many points does Miguel score?

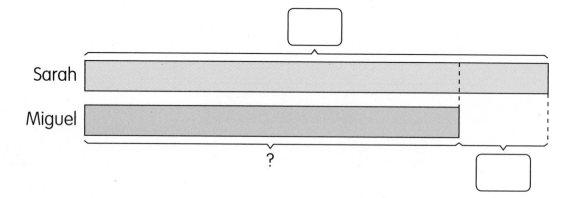

_____ ◯ _____ = _____

Miguel scores _____ points.

INDEPENDENT PRACTICE

Solve.
Use the bar model to help you.

1 Eli collected 37 toy trucks.
Michelle collected 66 more toy trucks than Eli.
How many toy trucks did Michelle collect?

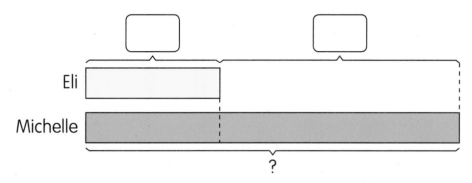

2 Kiara has 86 markers.
Dae has 49 fewer markers than Kiara.
How many markers does Dae have?

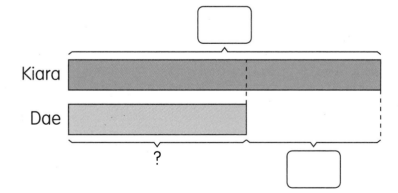

Solve.
Draw a bar model to help you.

3 108 children were wearing hats.
26 more children were not wearing hats than those who were.
How many children were **not** wearing hats?

4 Mr. Lewis baked 166 cherry pies.
He baked 77 more cherry pies than apple pies.
How many apple pies did he bake?

5 Paula made 123 masks.
Jose made 87 fewer masks than Paula.
How many masks did Jose make?

6 Mia picked 243 tomatoes.
Caleb picked 157 more tomatoes than Mia.
How many tomatoes did Caleb pick?

7 Bakery A baked 469 pies.
Bakery A baked 255 fewer pies than Bakery B.
How many pies did Bakery B bake?

8 There were 952 children watching a musical.
There were 265 fewer adults than children watching the musical.
How many adults were watching the musical?

Real-World Problems: Two-Step Problems

Learning Objective:
• Use bar models to solve two-step addition and subtraction real-world problems.

THINK

Payton has 10 more tickets than Cole.
After Payton gives 5 tickets to Cole, Cole has 25 tickets.
The number of tickets Cole has is the same as the number of tickets Payton has.
How many tickets does Payton have at first?

ENGAGE

Study the two bar models.

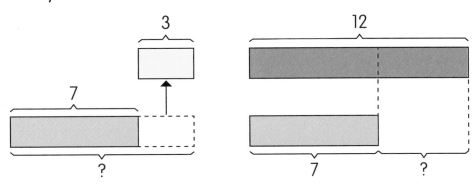

Share a story for each bar model with your partner.

Tell your partner why each bar model fits the story.

LEARN Solve two-step real-world problems involving addition and subtraction

1 There are 26 adults and 19 children at a park.
Later, 7 people leave the park.

   a   How many people are at the park at first?
   b   How many people are at the park now?

STEP 1 Understand the problem.

How many adults and how many children are there? What do I need to find?

STEP 2 Think of a plan.
I can draw a model.

STEP 3 Carry out the plan.

a
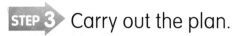

$26 + 19 = 45$

There are 45 people at the park at first.

b
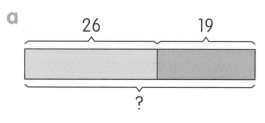

$45 - 7 = 38$

There are 38 people at the park now.

STEP 4 Check the answer.
I can work backwards from my answer.

$45 - 19 = 26$
My answer is correct.

$38 + 7 = 45$
My answer is correct.

TRY Practice solving two-step real-world problems involving addition and subtraction

Solve.
Use the bar model to help you.

1 There are 22 children and 16 adults on Bus A.
There are 5 more people on Bus B than on Bus A.

   a   How many people are there on Bus A?
   b   How many people are there on Bus B?

a

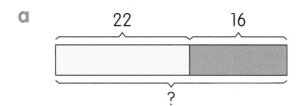

Are there more or fewer people on Bus A?

_____ ◯ _____ = _____

There are _____ people on Bus A.

b

_____ ◯ _____ = _____

There are _____ people on Bus B.

2 Mr. Brook gives out 341 posters to his students.
Ms. Garcia gives out 279 more posters than Mr. Brook.

   a   How many posters does Ms. Garcia give out?

   b   How many posters do both of them give out in all?

a

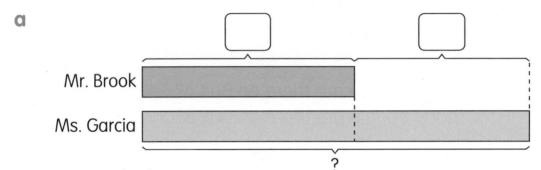

_____ ◯ _____ = _____

Ms. Garcia gives out _____ posters.

b

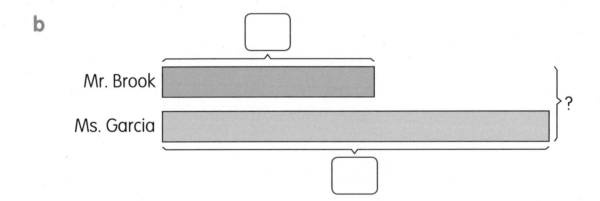

_____ ◯ _____ = _____

Both of them give out _____ posters in all.

3 Anna has 264 crayons and markers in all.
She has 93 markers.

    a   How many crayons does she have?

    b   How many more crayons than markers does she have?

a

Do I add or subtract?

_____ ◯ _____ = _____

She has _____ crayons.

b

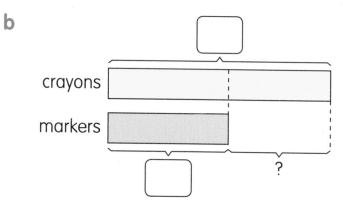

_____ ◯ _____ = _____

She has _____ more crayons than markers.

4 Angel has 345 counters.
She gives Aiden 78 counters.
Now, Angel has 183 blue counters and some red counters.
How many red counters does Angel have now?

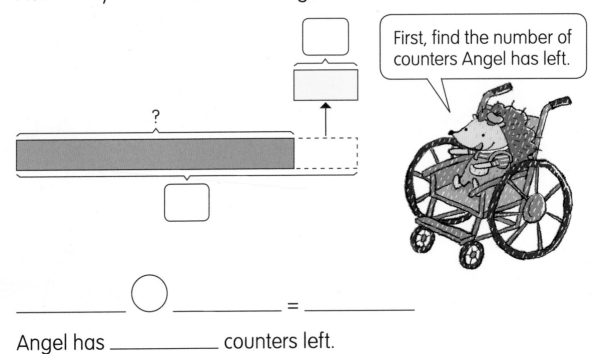

First, find the number of counters Angel has left.

_____ ◯ _____ = _____

Angel has _____ counters left.

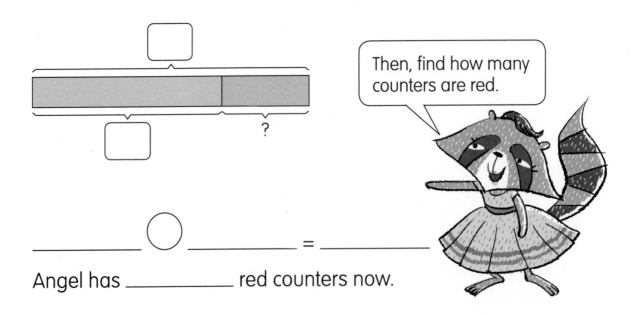

Then, find how many counters are red.

_____ ◯ _____ = _____

Angel has _____ red counters now.

5 Charles thinks of three numbers.
The first number is 504.
The second number is 148 less than the first number.
The third number is 57 more than the second number.
What is the third number?

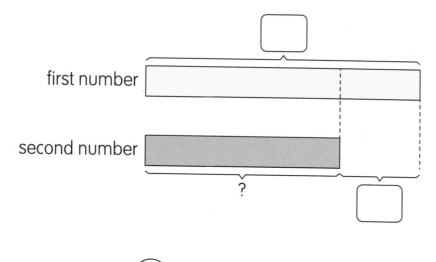

_____ ◯ _____ = _____

The second number is _____.

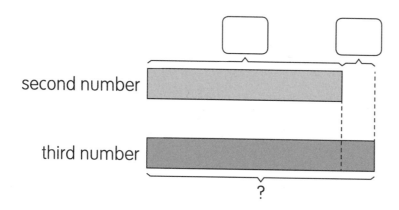

_____ ◯ _____ = _____

The third number is _____.

Work in pairs.
Read the problem.
Then, answer each question.

Amirah collected 120 seashells.
She collected fewer seashells than Andrew.
How many seashells did Andrew collect?

What information do I know?
What do I need to find out?

1 Give a few possible answers to the problem.

2 What are a few numbers that cannot be the possible answers? Why?

INDEPENDENT PRACTICE

Solve.
Use the bar model to help you.

1   A grocer had 78 coconuts and 130 peaches.
    After selling some peaches, he had 159 coconuts and peaches left.

    a   How many coconuts and peaches did the grocer have at first?
    b   How many peaches did the grocer sell?

    a

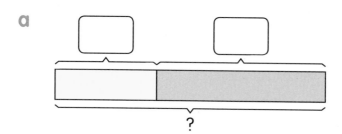

    b

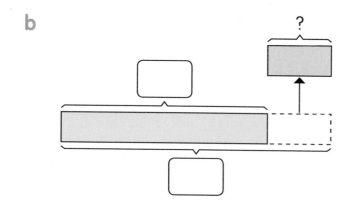

Solve.
Draw a bar model to help you.

2 784 people went hiking.
325 of the hikers were children and the rest were adults.

  a How many adults went hiking?
  b How many more adults than children were there?

  a

  b

3 356 adults went on a trip.
There were 192 more children than adults on the trip.
How many people went on the trip?

4 There are 245 toys in a store.
There are 36 dolls and 78 toy cars.
The rest are toy animals.
How many toy animals are there in the store?

Name: _____ Date: _____

Mathematical Habit 4 Use mathematical models

Read the problem.

A garden has 250 flowers.
90 of the flowers are roses and the rest are lilies.
Use the information above to write two questions.

1 _____

2 _____

Read the problem.

A bookstore has 468 books and magazines.
279 of them are books and the rest are magazines.
Use the information above to write two questions.

1 _____

2 _____

Problem Solving with Heuristics

1 **Mathematical Habit 4** **Use mathematical models**

Ms. Miller buys some watermelons for her restaurant.
She uses 15 watermelons.
Then, she buys 37 more watermelons.
Ms. Miller has 96 watermelons now.
How many watermelons does she have at first?

She has _____ watermelons at first.

2 **Mathematical Habit 4** **Use mathematical models**

Amari has 24 more stickers than Sophia.
Juan has 24 fewer stickers than Sophia.
How many more stickers does Amari have than Juan?

Amari has _____ more stickers than Juan.

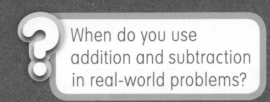

When do you use addition and subtraction in real-world problems?

Using Bar Models: Addition and Subtraction

Using Part-Whole

Adding On and Taking Away Sets

Comparing Two Sets

Solving Real-World Problems

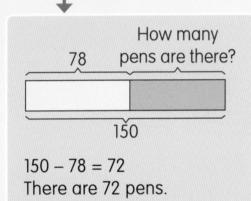

How many pens are there?

78

150

150 − 78 = 72
There are 72 pens.

a

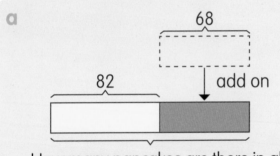

68

82

add on

How many pancakes are there in all?

82 + 68 = 150
There are 150 pancakes in all.

b

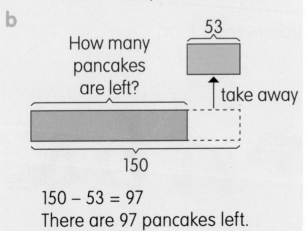

How many pancakes are left?

53

take away

150

150 − 53 = 97
There are 97 pancakes left.

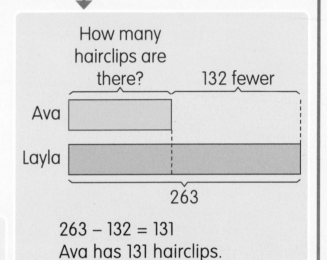

How many hairclips are there?

132 fewer

Ava

Layla

263

263 − 132 = 131
Ava has 131 hairclips.

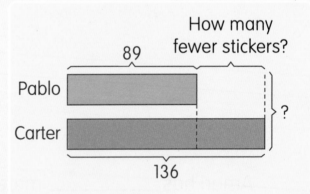

How many fewer stickers?

89

Pablo

Carter

?

136

a 136 − 89 = 47
Pablo has 47 fewer stickers than Carter.

b 89 + 136 = 225
They have 225 stickers in all.

Name: _____ Date: _____

Solve.
Draw a bar model to help you.

1 A farmer has 88 green apples and 54 red apples.
   How many apples does he have in all?

2 Wyatt has 100 hats in his store.
   25 of the hats are straw hats.
   The rest are sports caps.
   How many of them are sports caps?

3. Addison collected 205 beads.
Her mother gave her another 299 beads.
How many beads does Addison have now?

4. 436 children went to a camp on Friday.
187 children left the camp on Saturday.
How many children stayed on at the camp through Saturday?

5 Aubrey made 64 gifts for her guests at her party.
She made 33 fewer gifts than Alex.
How many gifts did Alex make?

6 Levi folded 75 paper planes to sell at a school fair.
He folded 36 fewer paper boats than paper planes.
How many paper planes and paper boats did he fold in all?

Assessment Prep

Answer each question.

7 Mr. Cooper planted 120 trees on his farm.
68 trees were pear trees.
23 trees were apple trees.
The rest were lemon trees.
How many lemon trees did he plant?

(A) 29

(B) 52

(C) 91

(D) 97

8 Make a ✓ in the box with the statement that describes the bar model correctly.

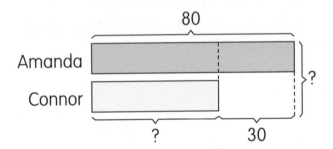

1	Amanda has 30 fewer toy cars than Connor.	
2	Connor has 50 toy cars.	
3	Connor has 30 fewer toy cars than Amanda.	
4	Amanda has 80 toy cars.	
5	Amanda and Connor have 130 toy cars in all.	

Name: _____ Date: _____

In a Restaurant

1 Gianna works in a restaurant.
She peeled 156 potatoes and 27 carrots.
How many vegetables did she peel in all?

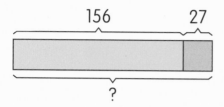

She peeled _____ vegetables in all.

2 There were 63 fish in a pond.
47 of the fish were goldfish.
The rest were guppies.
How many guppies were there in the pond?

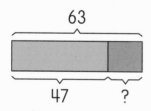

There were _____ guppies in the pond.

3 Tiana washed 56 plates in her restaurant.
Her father washed 183 plates in the restaurant.

a How many fewer plates did Tiana wash than her father?

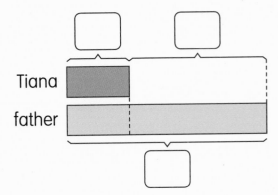

Tiana washed _____ fewer plates than her father.

b How many plates did they wash in all?

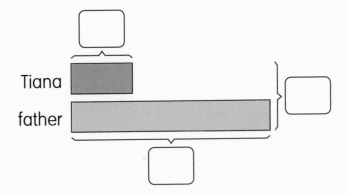

They washed _____ plates in all.

4 **a** Ms. Clark has 251 red rubber bands and 128 green rubber bands.
How many rubber bands does she have in all?
Draw a bar model to help you.

She has _____ rubber bands in all.

b There are 256 people in a restaurant.
123 of the people are adults.
The rest are children.
How many children are in the restaurant?

There are _____ children in the restaurant.

Rubric

Point(s)	Level	My Performance
7–8	4	• Most of my answers are correct. • I show all my work correctly. • I explain my thinking clearly and completely.
5–6.5	3	• Some of my answers are correct. • I show some of my work correctly. • I explain my thinking clearly.
3–4.5	2	• A few of my answers are correct. • I show little work correctly. • I explain some of my thinking clearly.
0–2.5	1	• A few of my answers are correct. • I show little or no work. • I do not explain my thinking clearly.

Teacher's Comments

Chapter
5 Length

My sandwich is about 6 inches long.

My sandwich is longer. It is about 1 foot long!

© 2020 Marshall Cavendish Education Pte Ltd

Given three objects, how can you find out which is longer?

Name: _____ Date: _____

Comparing lengths using a start line

Strip A

Strip B

Strip C

Start line

Strip A is shorter than Strip C.
Strip B is shorter than Strip A.
So, Strip B is shorter than Strip C.

Strip B is the shortest.
Strip C is the longest.

▶ Quick Check

Look at the picture.
Fill in each blank.
Use the words in the box.

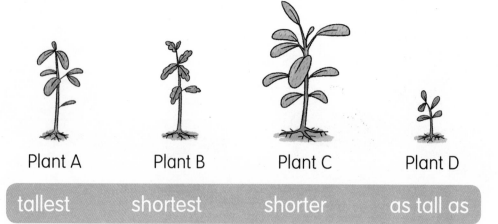

Plant A   Plant B   Plant C   Plant D

| tallest | shortest | shorter | as tall as |

1 Plant A is _____ Plant B.

2 Plant B is _____ than Plant C.

3 Plant D is the _____.

4 Plant C is the _____.

Measuring lengths in units

Each  stands for 1 unit.

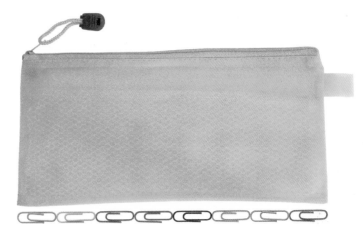

The pencil is about
5 units long.
The length of the pencil
is about 5 units.

The pencil case is about
8 units long.
The length of the pencil case
is about 8 units.

The pencil case is longer than the pencil.
The pencil is shorter than the pencil case.

▶ **Quick Check**

Fill in each blank.
Each  **stands for 1 unit.**

5

The diary is about _____ units long.

6

The ribbon is about _____ units long.

Use to measure.
Then, fill in each blank.
Each stands for 1 unit.

Leaf A

Leaf B

Leaf C

7 Leaf _____ is the shortest leaf.

It is about _____ units long.

8 Leaf _____ is the longest leaf.

It is about _____ units long.

9 Leaf C is longer than Leaf _____ and shorter than Leaf _____.

Leaf C is about _____ units long.

Measuring in Meters

Learning Objective:
* Measure and estimate length, width, and height in meters.

New Vocabulary
meter stick
length
meter (m)
width
height

 **THINK**

Without measuring, Ava guessed that a rope was about 7 meters long. What could the possible lengths of the rope be?

ENGAGE

1. Use a meter stick to measure your partner's height.
   Now, measure your partner's foot length.
   How do they compare?

2. Find the length of the teacher's desk.
   Share how you can measure the length in two ways.

LEARN Use a meter stick to measure length

1.

A meter stick is a tool used to measure the length of objects. The baseball bat is about 1 meter long.

|← ———————— 1 m ———————— →|

The **meter** is a unit of length.
m stands for meter.
Read 1 m as one meter.
Meter is used to measure longer lengths.

The length of the pair of pants is shorter than 1 meter.

The length of the walking cane is about 1 meter.

The length of the shovel is longer than 1 meter.

2

How wide is the cabinet?
The **width** of the cabinet is about 1 meter.

How high is the cabinet?
The **height** of the cabinet is about 2 meters.

Work in pairs.

(1) Use a meter stick to measure your arm span.
Is your arm span longer than or shorter than 1 meter?

My arm span is _____ than 1 meter.

(2) Guess the length of each object below.

(3) Use the meter stick to measure the lengths of the objects.

	My guess is	The length is about
The height of your classroom door	about 2 meters	
The width of your classroom door		
The length of your desk		
The length of your teacher's desk		

TRY Practice using a meter stick to measure length

Look at the pictures.
Write longer or shorter.

1 Meter sticks are placed below two noticeboards.

Noticeboard A   Noticeboard B

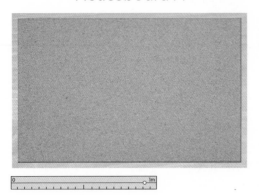 

a   Noticeboard A is _____ than 1 meter.

b   Noticeboard B is _____ than 2 meters.

Fill in each blank.

2 Name two objects in your school that are about

a   1 meter long. _____

b   1 meter wide. _____

c   1 meter high. _____

INDEPENDENT PRACTICE

Use a meter stick to measure.
Then, answer each question.

1 Is your classroom window longer or shorter than 1 meter?

_____

2 Name an object that is shorter than 1 meter.

_____

3 Name an object that is longer than 1 meter.

_____

4 Write the names of five objects in the chart.
Measure the lengths of the objects.
Then, make a ✓ in the correct box.

Object	Less than 1 meter	About 1 meter	More than 1 meter

Look at each picture.
Fill in each blank.

5

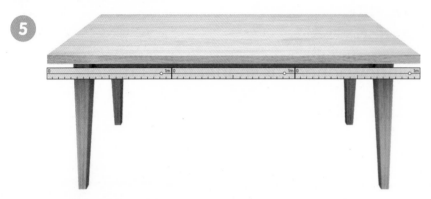

The table is about _____ meters long.

6

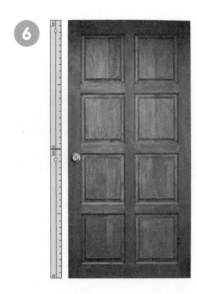

The door is about _____ meters high.

7

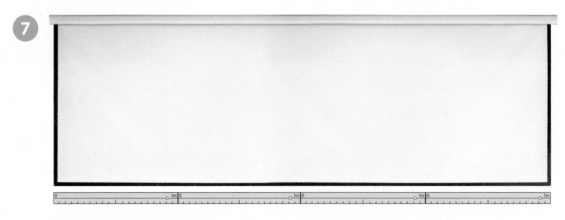

The screen is about _____ meters long.

Name: _____ Date: _____

Measuring in Centimeters

Learning Objectives:
- Measure and estimate length, width, and height in centimeters.
- Draw lines of given lengths in centimeters.

> **New Vocabulary**
> centimeter (cm)

 **THINK**

Emma's ruler was broken as shown below.
How can she use it to draw a line 10 centimeters long?

ENGAGE

1 Place your centimeter ruler along the pencil below.
What is the length of the pencil?
Share how you measured its length with your partner.

Now, measure the length of your pencil.
What is its length?

2 Ravi and Jayla measured the same pencil.
Ravi found it to be 9 centimeters long.
Jayla found it to be 6 centimeters long.
The actual length of the pencil is 7 centimeters.
What are the possible ways Ravi and Jayla measured the pencil?

LEARN Use a **centimeter** ruler to measure length

1 This is a centimeter ruler.

The lengths between the centimeter markings are equal.

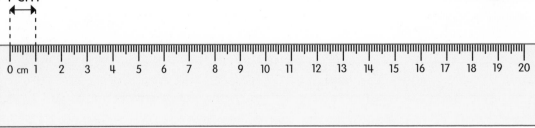

1 cm

The centimeter is a unit of length.
cm stands for centimeter.
Read 1 cm as one centimeter.
Centimeter is used to measure shorter lengths.

The width of your fingernail is about 1 centimeter.

2 You can use a centimeter ruler to find the length of shorter objects.

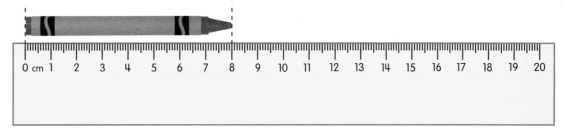

Place the crayon above the zero mark on the ruler.

Read the marking on the ruler where the crayon ends.

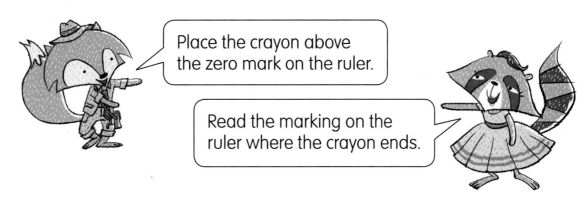

The length of the crayon is 8 centimeters.

3 What is the length of the piece of string?

Read the markings on the centimeter ruler to find out.

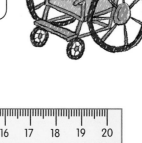

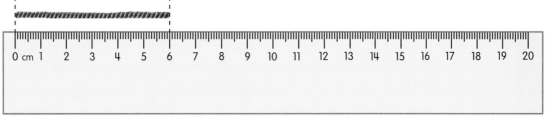

The length of the piece of string is 6 centimeters.

4 **What is the length of the sharpener?**

Oh no! My ruler is broken. How can I use it to find the length of the sharpener?

You can subtract to find the length of the sharpener.
$8 - 5 = 3$
The sharpener is 3 centimeters long.

Math Talk

The length of the pencil is 12 centimeters because it ends at the 12 centimeters mark.

Do you agree?
Why or why not?

Work in pairs.

① Your teacher will provide you with a strip of paper.
Use a centimeter ruler to measure its length.

The length of the strip is _____ centimeters.

② Use the strip to estimate the length of each object.

③ Use a centimeter ruler to find the length of each object.

	Estimated Length	Measured Length
The length of a paper clip		
The length of your eraser		
The width of your notebook		
The height of your pencil case		

TRY Practice using a centimeter ruler to measure length

Find the length of each object.

1

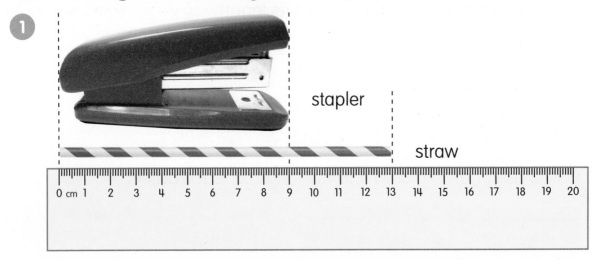

stapler

straw

a   The stapler is _____ centimeters long.

b   The straw is _____ centimeters long.

Measure the length of a line.
Use a centimeter ruler.

2 _____ Its length is _____ centimeters.

Use a centimeter ruler to draw.

3 a   Draw a line 4 centimeters long.

b   Draw a line 5 centimeters longer than the above.

Find the length of each object.

4   hairclip

    ribbon

0 cm 1 2 3 4 5 6 7 8 9 10 11 12 13 14 15 16 17 18 19 20

a   The ribbon is _____ centimeters long.

b   The hairclip is _____ centimeters long.

ENGAGE

Place a piece of string around the middle of a ball.
Mark the length with a pen.
Now, measure the length using a centimeter ruler
or a centimeter tape.
What is the length around the middle of the ball?

LEARN Use a centimeter tape to measure length

1

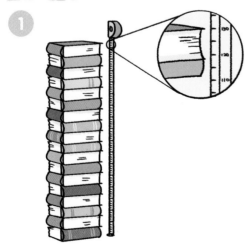

The stack of books is exactly 130 centimeters high.

2

The length around his head is 48 centimeters.

3 Look at the curve below.

How do you measure this curve?

Use a piece of string to trace the curve.
Then, measure the length of the string along a centimeter tape.

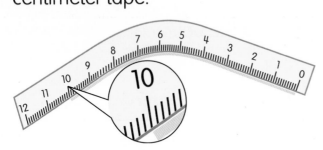

The string is 10 centimeters long.
So, the curve is 10 centimeters long.

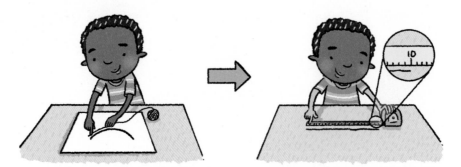

Work in pairs.

① Find two objects in the classroom.
Write the names of the objects you found.

	Object	The length around the object is
1		
2		

② Ask your partner to use a centimeter tape to measure the length around each object.
Then, write the lengths in the table above.

③ Compare the lengths.
Which object has a longer length around it? _____

④ Trade places. Repeat ① to ③.

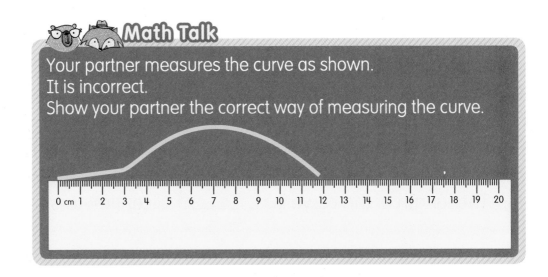

Math Talk

Your partner measures the curve as shown.
It is incorrect.
Show your partner the correct way of measuring the curve.

TRY Practice using a centimeter tape to measure length

Look at the picture.
Fill in each blank.

1. The bag is _____ centimeters long.

2. The bag is _____ centimeters wide.

Measure the length of each curve.
Use a piece of string and a centimeter tape to help you.

3.

The length of the curve is _____ centimeters.

4.

The length of the curve is _____ centimeters.

INDEPENDENT PRACTICE

Find the length of each object.

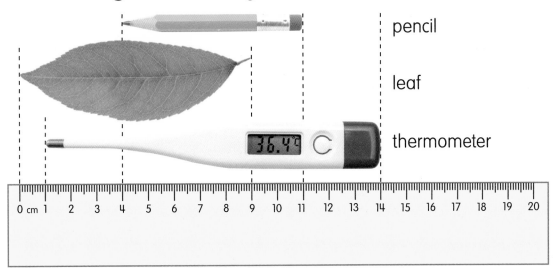

pencil

leaf

thermometer

1 The leaf is _____ centimeters long.

2 The pencil is _____ centimeters long.

3 The thermometer is _____ centimeters long.

Measure the length of each line.
Use a centimeter ruler.

4 _____

The line is _____ centimeters long.

5 _____

The line is _____ centimeters long.

Use a centimeter ruler to draw.

6 Draw a line 8 centimeters long.

7 Draw a line 3 centimeters shorter than the above.

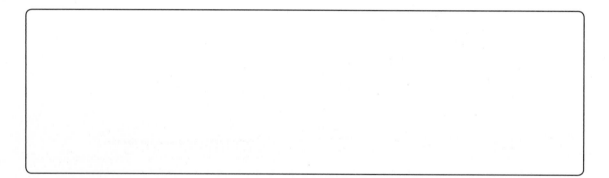

Measure the length of the curve.
Use a piece of string and a centimeter tape to help you.

8

The length of the curve is _____ centimeters.

3 Comparing and Ordering Metric Lengths

Learning Objectives:
- Compare and order metric lengths.
- Find the difference in lengths of objects in metric units.

THINK

Zoey has three threads.
Thread A and Thread B measure 33 centimeters in all.
Thread B and Thread C measure 38 centimeters in all.
Thread A, Thread B and Thread C measure a total of 53 centimeters.
Find the length of each thread.
Then, order the threads from shortest to longest.

Which thread is the shortest?
Which thread is the longest?
How do you know?

ENGAGE

Michelle, Callia, and Lucy have a piece of string each.
Michelle's string is 3 meters longer than Callia's string.
Callia's string is 9 meters long.
What is the length of Michelle's string?
Lucy's string is 5 meters shorter than Michelle's string.
Order the pieces of string from shortest to longest.
Share how you ordered the pieces of string with your partner.

LEARN Use meters to compare and order lengths

1 Ms. Brown, Mr. Lopez, and Ms. Lee have fences around their yards.
How can you find out whose fence is the tallest?

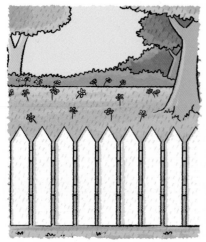

Ms. Brown's fence

Mr. Lopez's fence

Ms. Lee's fence

I cannot tell which fence is taller because I cannot put them side by side.

You can compare by using a meter stick.

TRY Practice using meters to compare and order lengths

Answer each question.

1. Ribbon A

   Ribbon B

   a   Which ribbon is longer? _____

   b   How much longer? _____ meters

2. Bailey has two ropes.
   Rope A is 12 meters long.
   Rope B is 8 meters long.

   a   Which rope is longer? _____

   b   How much longer is it? _____ meters

3. Ship A is 362 meters long.
   Ship B is 399 meters long.
   Ship C is 360 meters long.

   a   Which ship is the longest? _____

   b   Which ship is the shortest? _____

   c   Order the ships from longest to shortest.

   _____   _____   _____
     longest   shortest

ENGAGE

Brandon's pencil is 2 centimeters shorter than Aika's pencil.
Carter's pencil is 6 centimeters longer than Brandon's pencil.
Draw a diagram to find the shortest and longest pencils.

LEARN Use centimeters to compare and order lengths

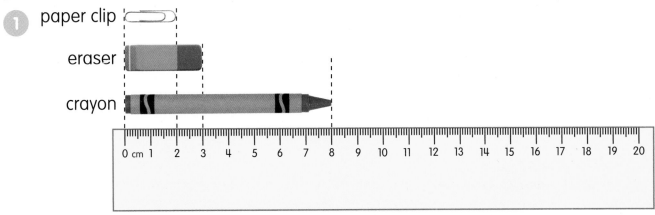

The paper clip is 2 centimeters long.
The eraser is 3 centimeters long.
The crayon is 8 centimeters long.

The eraser is longer than the paper clip.
3 – 2 = 1
It is 1 centimeter longer.

The crayon is longer than the eraser.
8 – 3 = 5
It is 5 centimeters longer.

The eraser is shorter than the crayon.
8 – 3 = 5
It is 5 centimeters shorter.

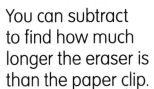

You can subtract to find how much longer the eraser is than the paper clip.

The paper clip is the shortest and the crayon is the longest.

Ordered from shortest to longest, the objects are:

paper clip	eraser	crayon
shortest		longest

Math Talk

Look at the picture.
Which is longer, the
eraser or the pen?
How much longer?

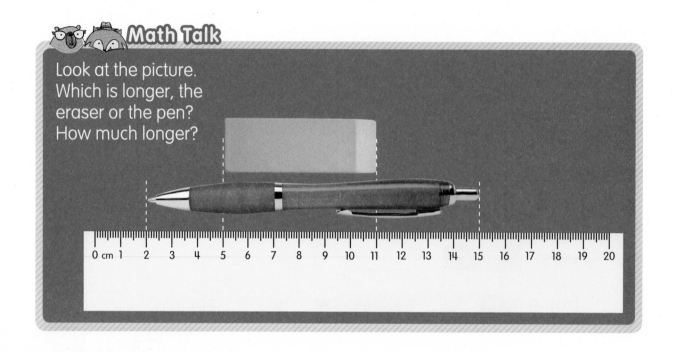

Hands-on Activity Using centimeters to compare and order lengths

Work in pairs.

1. Choose the unit of length to use for measuring each object.
Tell your classmate why you choose meter or centimeter.

	My guess is (m or cm)	The length is about
The height of your desk leg		
The length of your eraser		
The length of your classroom whiteboard		
The length of your pencil		
The height of your partner		

2. Guess the length of each object.
Use m or cm as the unit of length.

3. Use a meter stick, centimeter ruler, or centimeter tape to measure each object.

TRY Practice using centimeters to compare and order lengths

Look at the picture.
Then, answer each question.

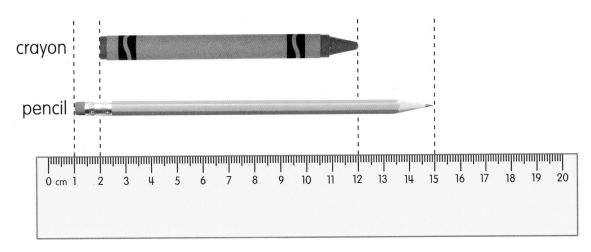

crayon

pencil

1 How long is the crayon?

_____ – _____ = _____

The crayon is _____ centimeters long.

> The crayon is placed between the 2 centimeters and the 12 centimeters mark. We subtract to find its length.

2 How long is the pencil?

_____ – _____ = _____

The pencil is _____ centimeters long.

3 How much longer is the pencil than the crayon?

_____ – _____ = _____

The pencil is _____ centimeters longer than the crayon.

Look at the picture.
Then, fill in each blank.

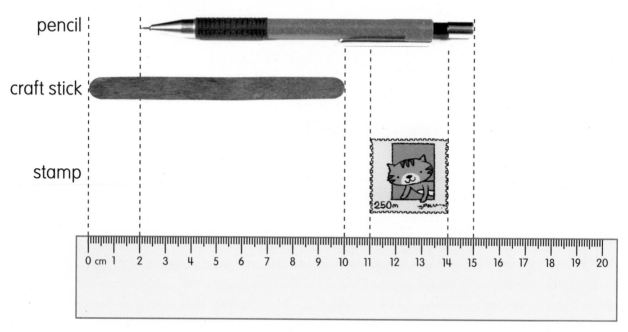

pencil

craft stick

stamp

4 How much shorter is the stamp than the craft stick?

_____ – _____ = _____

The stamp is _____ centimeters shorter than the craft stick.

5 How much longer is the pencil than the craft stick?

_____ – _____ = _____

The pencil is _____ centimeters longer than the craft stick.

6 Order the objects from shortest to longest.

_____ _____ _____
shortest   longest

The stamp is placed between the 11 centimeters mark and the 14 centimeters mark. What is the length of the stamp?

INDEPENDENT PRACTICE

Answer each question.

1 Which tree is shorter? _____

2 The length of an ice skating rink is 25 meters.
The length of a swimming pool is 50 meters.

Which is longer? _____

ice skating rink

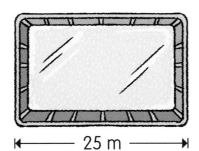

swimming pool

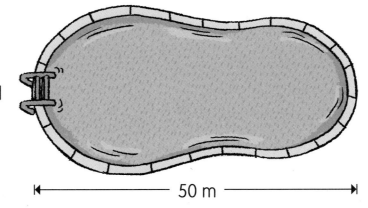

Use the picture to answer each question.

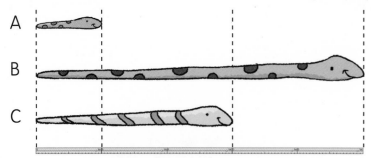

A

B

C

3 Which is the longest snake? _____

4 Order the snakes from shortest to longest.

_____ _____ _____
   shortest   longest

Use the picture to answer each question.

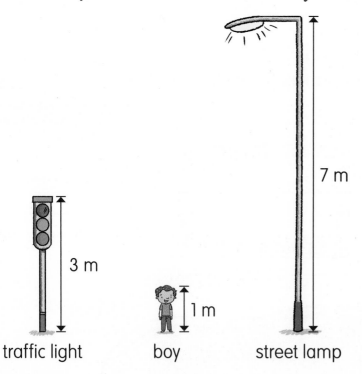

7 m

3 m

1 m

traffic light   boy   street lamp

5 Which is the tallest? _____

6 Order them from tallest to shortest.

_____ _____ _____
   tallest   shortest

Use a centimeter tape and a piece of string to measure.
Then, answer the question.

toothbrush

yarn

7 Which is longer, the toothbrush or the yarn?

The _____ is longer.

Use a centimeter ruler to measure each length.
Then, answer each question.

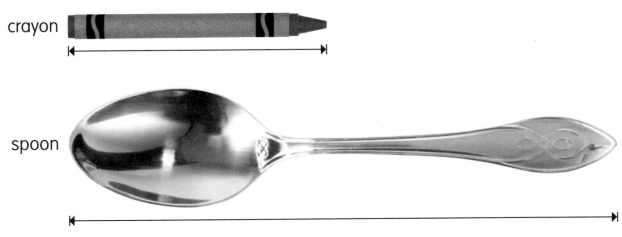

crayon

spoon

8 How long is the crayon? _____ centimeters

9 How long is the spoon? _____ centimeters

10 Which is longer? _____

How much longer? _____ centimeter

Use the picture to answer each question.

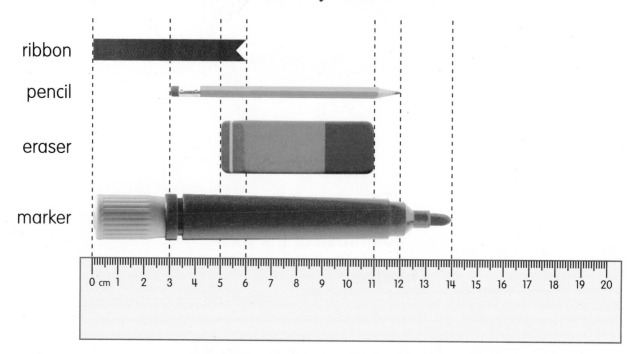

⑪ What is the length of the marker? _____ centimeters

⑫ Which is longer, the pencil or the marker? _____
How much longer? _____ centimeters

⑬ The longest item is the _____.

⑭ The _____ and the _____ have the same length.

4 Real-World Problems: Addition and Subtraction of Metric Lengths

Learning Objective:
• Solve one-step and two-step real-world problems involving metric lengths.

THINK

Ryan has 18 meters of cloth.
He has 6 meters of cloth more than Elena.
How much cloth must Elena give to Ryan so that Ryan's cloth is double the length of Elena's?

What information do I know?
What do I need to find out?

ENGAGE

a   Luke has a red string and a blue string.
The red string is 5 centimeters long.
The blue string is 4 centimeters long.

b   Use the information to complete the bar model.

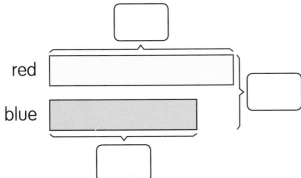

red

blue

Think of two questions you can ask using the bar model.
Share your questions with your partner.

LEARN Solve one-step real-world problems involving addition and subtraction of metric lengths

1 Dara walks for 10 meters and jogs for another 6 meters. How many meters does Dara walk and jog in all?

STEP 1 Understand the problem.

How many meters does Dara walk?
How many meters does Dara jog?
What do I need to find?

STEP 2 Think of a plan.
I can draw a bar model.

STEP 3 Carry out the plan.

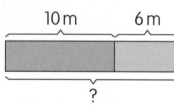

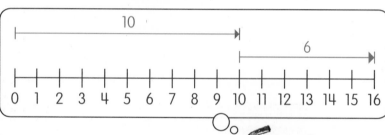

$10 + 6 = 16$

Dara walks and jogs 16 meters in all.

STEP 4 Check the answer.
I can work backwards to check my answer.

$16 - 6 = 10$

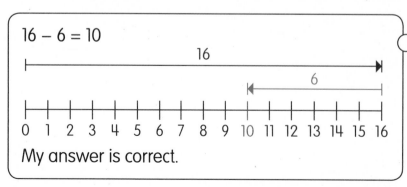

My answer is correct.

2 Diego has a piece of cloth.
It is 25 centimeters long.
He cuts it into two pieces.
The first piece is 17 centimeters long.
What is the length of the second piece?

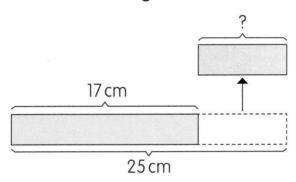

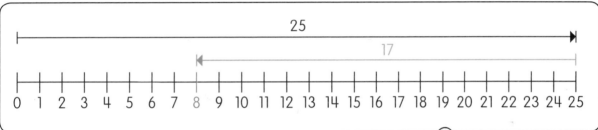

$25 - 17 = 8$

The length of the second piece
is 8 centimeters.

TRY Practice solving one-step real-world problems involving addition and subtraction of metric lengths

Solve.
Use the bar model to help you.

1

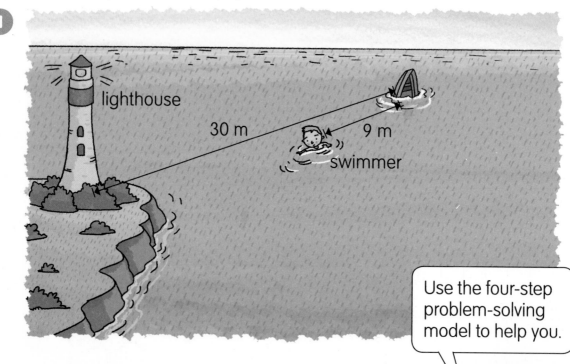

lighthouse

30 m

9 m

swimmer

Use the four-step problem-solving model to help you.

How far is the swimmer from the lighthouse?

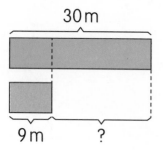

30 m

9 m   ?

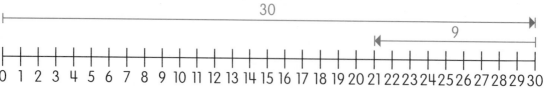

30

9

0 1 2 3 4 5 6 7 8 9 10 11 12 13 14 15 16 17 18 19 20 21 22 23 24 25 26 27 28 29 30

_____ ◯ _____ = _____

The swimmer is _____ meters from the lighthouse.

2

store

playground

Grace's house

80 m

421 m

Grace walks from her house to the store.
On her way, she passes by the playground.
How far does she walk in all?

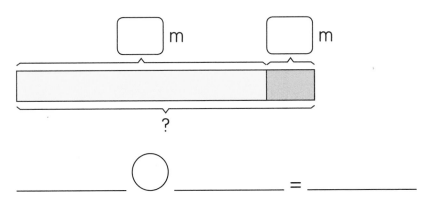

3 Riley took part in a 100-meter race.
She ran 36 meters, then she tripped and fell.
How far away was she from the finish line when she fell?

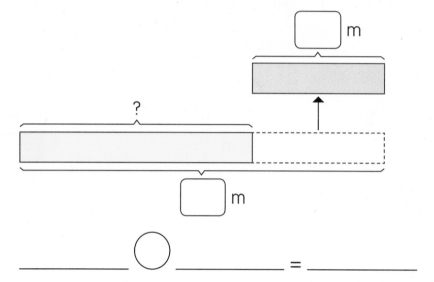

_____ ◯ _____ = _____

She was _____ meters away from the finish line when she fell.

4 Tyler has a piece of cloth that is 75 meters long.
Kate gives him another 86 meters of cloth.
What is the total length of cloth that Tyler has now?

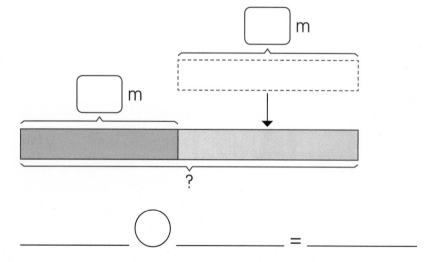

_____ ◯ _____ = _____

The total length of cloth that Tyler has now is _____ meters.

a   Liam has 50 centimeters of ribbon.
Emily has 27 centimeters of ribbon.
How much more ribbon does Liam have than Emily?
How much ribbon do they have in all?
Draw a bar model to show your thinking.

b   What is the least length of ribbon Liam must give Emily, so that she has a longer length of ribbon than Liam?

LEARN Solve two-step real-world problems involving addition and subtraction of metric lengths

1   Sara has a cloth that is 28 centimeters long.
She cuts it into three pieces.
The first piece is 12 centimeters long.
The second piece is 9 centimeters long.

   a   Find the total length of the first and second pieces.

   b   What is the length of the third piece?

   a

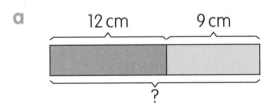

$$12 + 9 = 21$$

The total length of the first and second pieces is 21 centimeters.

b

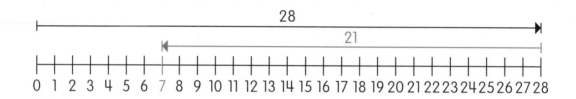

$28 - 21 = 7$

The length of the third piece is 7 centimeters.

TRY Practice solving two-step real-world problems involving addition and subtraction of metric lengths

Solve.
Use the bar model to help you.

1. Mr. Reed used 8 meters of cloth to make some curtains.
He used another 5 meters of cloth to make a dress.
Mr. Reed was left with 11 meters of cloth.
Find the length of cloth he had at first.

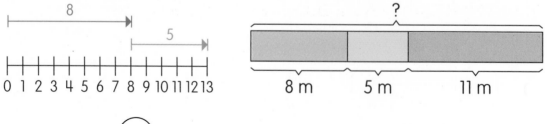

_____ ◯ _____ = _____

He used _____ meters of cloth in all.

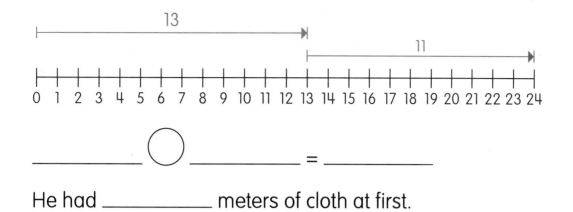

_____ ◯ _____ = _____

He had _____ meters of cloth at first.

2 Kayla has a red ribbon 100 centimeters long.
She cuts 36 centimeters off the ribbon.
Then, she joins a blue ribbon, 75 centimeters long,
to the remaining red ribbon.
What is the total length of the ribbon now?

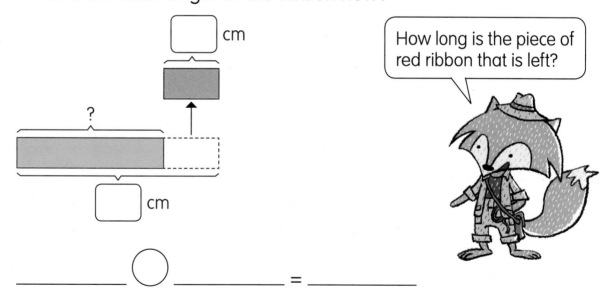

_____ ◯ _____ = _____

The length of the red ribbon she has left is

_____ centimeters.

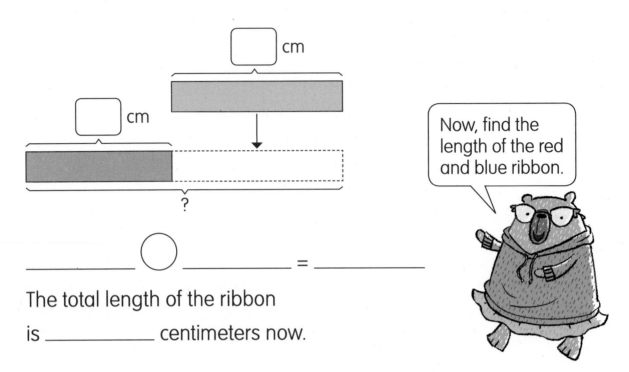

_____ ◯ _____ = _____

The total length of the ribbon

is _____ centimeters now.

Now, find the length of the red and blue ribbon.

3 Maya and Alan walked a total of 205 meters.
Maya walked 149 meters.
How much more did Maya walk than Alan?

First, find the distance Alan walked.

_____ ◯ _____ = _____

Alan walked _____ meters.

_____ ◯ _____ = _____

Maya walked _____ meters more than Alan.

Now, find how much more Maya walked.

INDEPENDENT PRACTICE

Solve.
Use the bar model to help you.

1 The length of Ella's notebook is 21 centimeters.
Austin's notebook is 5 centimeters longer.
What is the length of Austin's notebook?

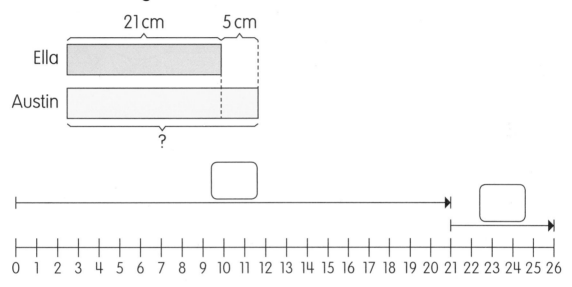

2 A piece of string that is 20 centimeters long is cut into two pieces.
One piece is 8 centimeters long.
How long is the other piece?

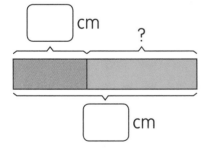

Solve.
Draw a bar model to help you.

③ Ang jogs two times around a 400-meter track.
How far does he jog in meters?

④ Claire's piece of string is 25 centimeters long.
Malik's piece of string is 12 centimeters longer.
How long is Malik's piece of string?

5 A tall room has two windows, one above the other.
The bottom window is 162 centimeters tall.
The top window is 47 centimeters shorter.

a How tall is the top window?

b What is the height of both windows?

6 A rope is 42 meters long.
It is cut into two pieces.
The first piece is 14 meters long.
How much longer is the second piece than the first piece?

© 2020 Marshall Cavendish Education Pte Ltd

5 Measuring in Feet

Learning Objective:
* Measure and estimate length, width, and height in feet.

THINK

Without measuring, Lydia guessed that her guitar was about 3 feet tall. What could the possible heights of her guitar be?

ENGAGE

Place a foot ruler beside a meter stick.
How do they compare?

Is 1 foot longer or shorter than 1 meter?

Is 1 centimeter longer or shorter than 1 foot?

How many foot rulers will be longer than a meter stick?

LEARN Use a foot ruler to measure length

1 Jasmine, Evan, and Lucas have a strip of cardboard each.
They use a foot ruler to measure the lengths.

The length of my cardboard strip is less than 1 foot.

The length of my strip is about 1 foot.

The length of my strip is more than 1 foot.

The ruler used for measurement is 1 foot long.
It is divided into 12 inches.

> The foot is a unit of length.
> ft stands for foot.
> Read 1 ft as one foot, and 2 ft as two feet.
> Foot is used to measure longer length.

2

The table is about 2 feet high.

The table is about 1 foot wide.

Work in pairs.

① Guess the length of each object in your classroom.

② Use a foot ruler to measure the length of each object.

	My guess is	The length is between
The length of your friend's arm	about 2 feet	2 feet and 3 feet
The width of your desk		
The height of your chair		
The height of your teacher's desk		
The length of the bookshelf		
The width of the window		
The width of your classroom		
The length of your classroom		

TRY Practice using a foot ruler to measure length

Use a foot ruler to measure.
Then, answer each question.

1 Is the flag pole at your school more than or less than 1 foot high?

The flag pole at my school is _____ 1 foot high.

2 Name two objects in your classroom that are about

   a   1 foot long. _____

   b   1 foot tall. _____

Fill in each blank.
Write more or less.

3

Box A

Box B

   a   Box A is _____ than 1 foot long.

   b   Box B is _____ than 2 feet long.

INDEPENDENT PRACTICE

Use a foot ruler to measure.
Then, answer each question.

1 Is the width of your classroom door more than or

less than 1 foot? _____

2 Is the height of the whiteboard more than or

less than 1 foot? _____

3 Is the length of your pencil case more than or

less than 1 foot? _____

4 Write the name of five objects in the chart.
Measure the lengths of the objects.
Then, make a ✓ in the correct box.

Object	Less than 1 foot	About 1 foot	More than 1 foot

Look at each picture.
Then, fill in each blank.

5

The book is about _____ foot long.

6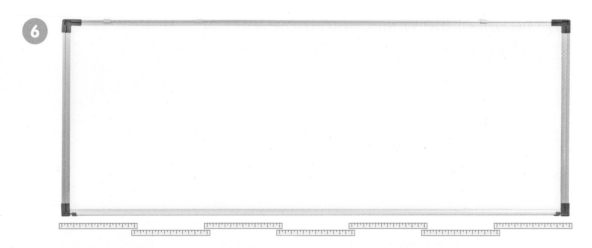

The whiteboard is about _____ feet long.

7

The chair is about _____ feet high.

 **Measuring in Inches**

Learning Objectives:
- Measure and estimate length, width, and height in inches.
- Draw lines of given lengths in inches.

> **New Vocabulary**
> inch (in.)

THINK

Daniel needs to paste a ribbon around a pole.
How can he measure the length of the ribbon he needs in inches?

ENGAGE

1 Use an inch ruler to measure the length of your thumb.
Is it longer or shorter than 1 foot?
How do you know?

2 Vijay has a ribbon longer than 2 inches but shorter than 7 inches.
Eli's ribbon is longer than Vijay's ribbon but less than 1 foot long.
What are the possible lengths of Eli's ribbon in inches?

LEARN Use an inch ruler to measure length

1 Inches are marked on this ruler.

The inch is a unit of length.
in. stands for inch.
Read 1 in. as one inch.
Inch is used to measure shorter lengths.

2 What is the length of the crayon?

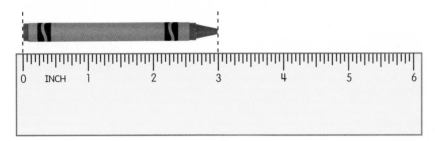

The length of the crayon starts at the 0 mark. It ends at the 3-inch mark. So, the length of the crayon is 3 inches.

3 What is the length of the paper clip?

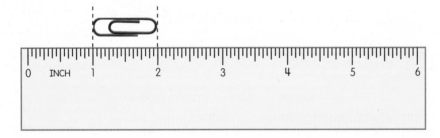

$2 - 1 = 1$

The paper clip is 1 inch long.

4 How long is the curve?

The string is 4 inches long.
So, the curve is 4 inches long.

🦉🦊 **Math Talk**

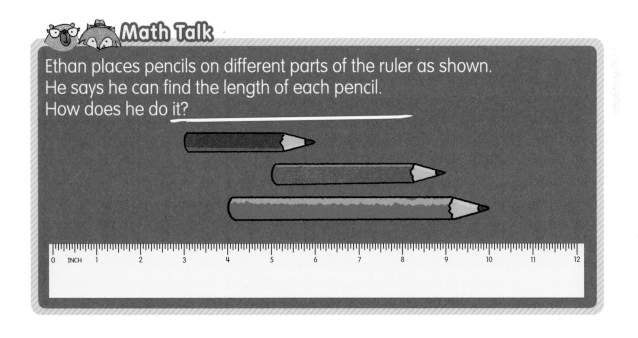

Ethan places pencils on different parts of the ruler as shown.
He says he can find the length of each pencil.
How does he do it?

Hands-on Activity Using an inch ruler to measure length

Work in pairs.

(1) Your teacher will provide you with a strip of paper. Use an inch ruler to measure its length.

The length of the strip is _____ inches.

(2) Use the strip to estimate the length of each object.

(3) Use an inch ruler to find the length of each object.

	Estimated Length	Measured Length
The length of a paper clip		
The length of your eraser		
The width of your notebook		
The height of your pencil case		

TRY Practice using an inch ruler to measure length

Use the inch ruler to find each missing number.

1. candle

   paper clip

   a   The length of the candle is _____ inches.

   b   The length of the paper clip is _____ inches.

2.

   a   The vase is about _____ inches long.

   b   The mouth of the vase is about _____ inches wide.

3. pen

   paintbrush

   a   How long is the pen?

   _____ − _____ = _____

   The pen is _____ inches long.

b How long is the paintbrush?

_____ – _____ = _____

The paintbrush is _____ inches long.

Measure the length of the curve.
Use a piece of string and an inch ruler to help you.

4

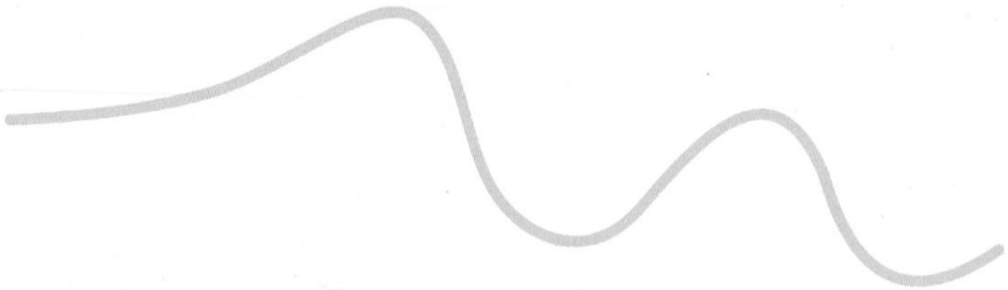

The length of the curve is _____ inches.

Use an inch ruler to draw.

5 **a** Draw a line 4 inches long.

b Draw a line 1 inch shorter than the above.

INDEPENDENT PRACTICE

Measure each line.
Use an inch ruler.

1 _____

Its length is _____ inches.

2 _____

Its length is _____ inches.

Use the inch ruler to find the missing number.

3

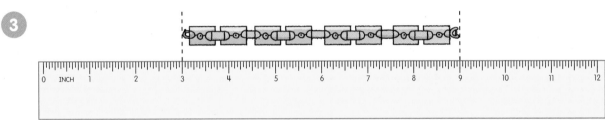

The bracelet is _____ inches long.

Measure the length of the curve.
Use a piece of string and an inch ruler to help you.

4 The length of the curve is _____ inches.

Use an inch ruler to draw.
Then, answer the question.

5 Draw a line 3 inches long.
Name it Line A.

6 Draw a line 2 inches longer than Line A.
Name it Line B.

7 Draw a line 1 inch shorter than Line B.
Name it Line C.

8 What is the length of Line C?

The length of Line C is _____ inches.

7 Comparing and Ordering Customary Lengths

Learning Objectives:
- Compare and order customary lengths.
- Find the difference in lengths of objects in customary units.
- Compare how lengths relate to the size of the unit.

THINK

Lola has three toy trains.
Train A is longer than Train B.
Train B is shorter than Train C.
Order the toy trains from shortest to longest.
Describe the steps you took to order the three toy trains.

> Which toy train is the shortest?
> Which toy train is the longest?
> How do you know?

ENGAGE

A tomato plant is 13 inches tall.
A pepper plant is shorter than the tomato plant.
A corn stalk is taller than the tomato plant.
Order the plants from tallest to shortest.
What are some possible heights of the plants?
Share your thinking with your partner.

LEARN Use feet and inches to compare and order lengths

1

My party bunting is 4 feet long.

Tomas

My party bunting is 5 feet long.
5 − 4 = 1
It is 1 foot longer than Tomas's party bunting.

Lauren

My party bunting is more than 6 feet long. It is the longest. Tomas's party bunting is the shortest.

Yong

2

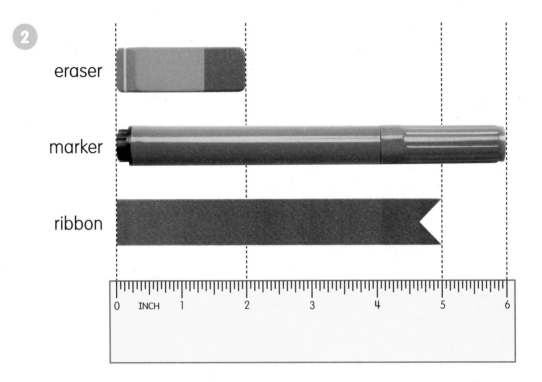

The eraser is 2 inches long.
The marker is 6 inches long.
The ribbon is 5 inches long.

The marker is longer than the eraser.
$6 - 2 = 4$
It is 4 inches longer.

The marker is longer than the ribbon.
$6 - 5 = 1$
It is 1 inch longer.

The eraser is shorter than the marker.
$6 - 2 = 4$
It is 4 inches shorter.

From shortest to longest, the objects are:

eraser	ribbon	marker
shortest		longest

You can subtract to find how much longer the marker is than the eraser.

TRY Practice using feet and inches to compare and order lengths

Use the foot rulers to answer each question.

Bookshelf A

Bookshelf B

1 Which bookshelf is longer?

Bookshelf _____ is longer.

2 How much longer is it?

_____ − _____ = _____

It is _____ foot longer.

Fill in each blank.

Jack makes two banners for his art class.
The red banner is 14 feet long.
The green banner is 22 feet long.

3 Which banner is shorter?

The _____ banner is shorter.

4 How much shorter is it?

_____ − _____ = _____

It is _____ feet shorter.

Look at the picture.
Then, fill in each blank.

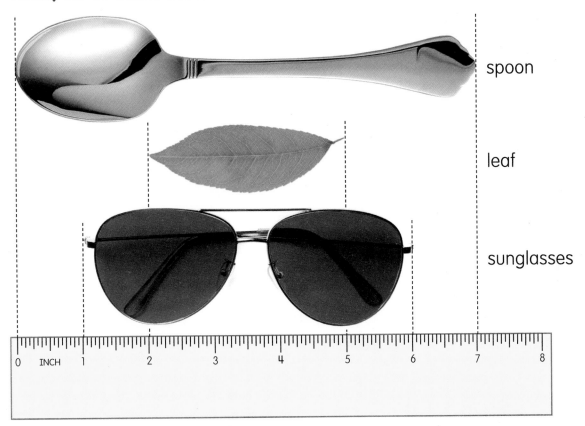

5 The pair of sunglasses is _____ inches long.

6 The leaf is _____ inches long.

7 The spoon is _____ inches long.

8 The pair of sunglasses is _____ inches longer than the leaf.

9 From longest to shortest, the objects are:

_____   _____   _____
   longest   shortest

1 Measure the length of your classroom whiteboard.
How many feet long is it?
How many inches long is it?
Which is an easier measure to use for a long object?
Share your thinking with your partner.

2 Correct the sentences if they are incorrect.
a   A cat is 2 inches tall.
b   It is 24 feet tall.

LEARN Compare inches to feet

1 Inches are used to measure shorter lengths.
Feet are used to measure longer lengths.

A 12-inch ruler is 1 foot long.

The laptop is about 12 inches long.
It is about 1 foot long.

An inch is shorter than a foot.
So, it takes more inches to
measure the laptop.

Math Talk

Bruno says his limb is about 2 feet long.
Lily says her thumb is about 2 inches long.
Which is longer, 2 feet or 2 inches?
Why?

Work in pairs.

① Measure each object in inches.
Then, measure it again in feet.

	Length in Inches	Length in Feet
The width of your teacher's desk		
The height of your chair		
The length of the board		
The height of the bookshelf		
The length of a book		

② Which objects are easier to measure using inches?

_____

③ Which objects are easier to measure using feet?

_____

④ Why are there more inches than feet when you measure the same object?

_____

TRY Practice comparing inches to feet

Fill in each blank.

1. Farrah measures the length of a box in both inches and feet.
    Will there be fewer inches or fewer feet?
    Why?

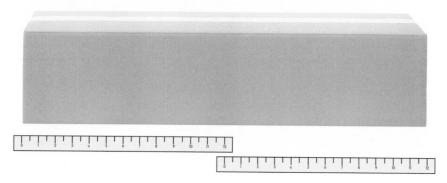

There will be fewer _____.

One _____ is longer than one _____.

2. A red ribbon is 3 feet long.
    A yellow ribbon is 3 inches long.
    Which ribbon is longer, the red or the yellow?
    Why?

The _____ ribbon is longer than the _____ ribbon.

The _____ is a longer unit of measure.

INDEPENDENT PRACTICE

Answer each question.

1 Which is longer, Rope A or Rope B?

Rope A

Rope B

_____ is longer.

2 The length of a toy car racetrack is 10 feet.
The length of a toy train is 15 feet.

a Which is longer? _____

b How much longer is it? _____ feet

Fill in each blank.

3 Gavin is 4 feet tall.
The monkey bars are 5 feet tall.
The flagpole is 20 feet tall.
From shortest to tallest, they are:

_____ _____ _____
shortest   tallest

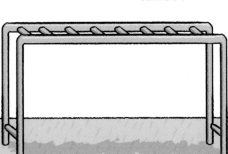

4

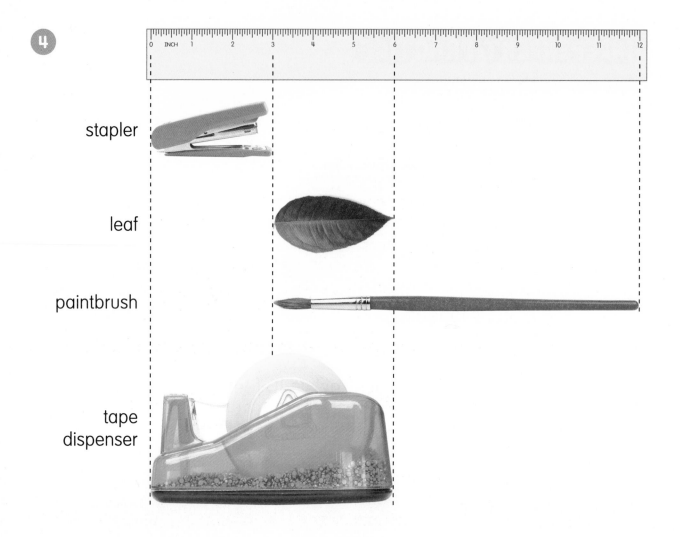

stapler

leaf

paintbrush

tape dispenser

a What is the length of the stapler? _____ inches

b Which is longer, the leaf or the tape dispenser? _____

c The longest item is the _____.

d Which two items have the same length?

   _____

5 Measure the height of a table using inches.
   Then, measure the height using feet.

   Did it take more inches or more feet to measure the height?

   Explain. _____

 8 Real-World Problems: Addition and Subtraction of Customary Lengths

Learning Objective:
• Solve one-step and two-step real-world problems involving customary lengths.

THINK

The total length of Pencil A and Pencil B is longer than the total length of Pencil A and Pencil C.

The total length of Pencil A and Pencil C is shorter than the total length of Pencil B and Pencil C.

Order the lengths of Pencils A, B, and C in two different ways.

Share how you ordered the pencils with your partner.

What information do I know?
What do I need to find out?

ENGAGE

The total length of Ellie's ribbon and Ivan's ribbon is shorter than the total length of Ellie's ribbon and Mai's ribbon.

Ellie's ribbon is longer than Mai's ribbon.

Ivan's ribbon is 8 centimeters shorter than Mai's ribbon.

Who has the longest ribbon?

Draw bar models to help you.

LEARN Solve real-world problems involving addition and subtraction of customary lengths

1 Alyssa walks 9 feet.
Then, she turns right and walks 17 feet.
How far does Alyssa walk in all?

STEP 1 Understand the problem.

How far does Alyssa walk at first?
How far does Alyssa walk after she turns right?
What do I need to find?

STEP 2 Think of a plan.
I can draw a bar model.

STEP 3 Carry out the plan.

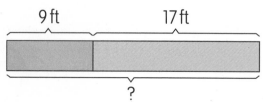

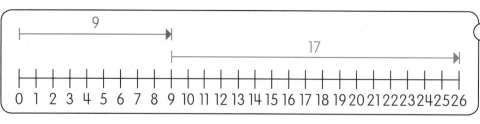

9 + 17 = 26

Alyssa walks 26 feet in all.

STEP 4 Check the answer.
I can work backwards to
check my answer.

26 − 17 = 9
My answer is correct.

© 2020 Marshall Cavendish Education Pte Ltd

2 Evelyn wraps gifts for her friends.
She cuts a 47-inch long strip of wrapping paper into 3 pieces.
The first piece is 14 inches long.
The second piece is 18 inches long.

    a   Find the total length of the first and second pieces.

    b   What is the length of the third piece?

    a

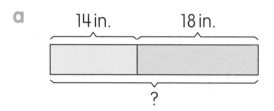

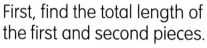
First, find the total length of the first and second pieces.

$14 + 18 = 32$

The total length of the first and second pieces is 32 inches.

    b

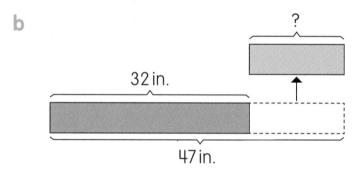

Now, find the length of the third piece.

$47 - 32 = 15$

The length of the third piece is 15 inches.

Practice solving real-world problems involving addition and subtraction of customary lengths

Solve.
Use the bar model to help you.

1

Boat B

6 ft

Boat A

20 ft

How far is the boy from the Boat A?

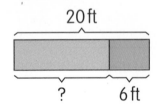

20 ft

?   6 ft

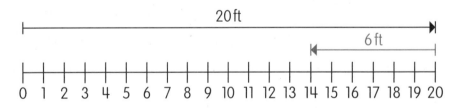

20 ft

6 ft

0 1 2 3 4 5 6 7 8 9 10 11 12 13 14 15 16 17 18 19 20

_____ ⃝ _____ = _____

The boy is _____ feet from Boat A.

2

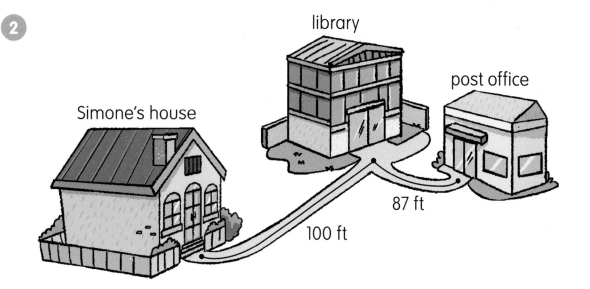

library

post office

Simone's house

87 ft

100 ft

Simone walks from her house to the post office to mail a package.
On her way, she passes the library.
How far does she walk in all?

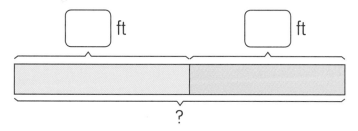

⬚ ft   ⬚ ft

?

_____ ◯ _____ = _____

She walks _____ feet in all.

3 Owen runs 800 feet.
John runs 637 feet.
How many feet more does Owen run than John?

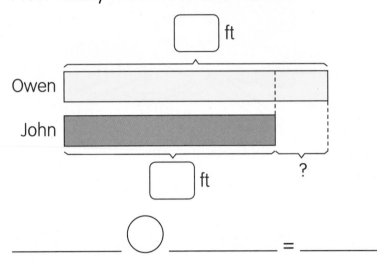

_____ ◯ _____ = _____

Owen runs _____ feet more than John.

4 Zane is 60 inches tall.
Kylie is 17 inches shorter.
What is their total height?

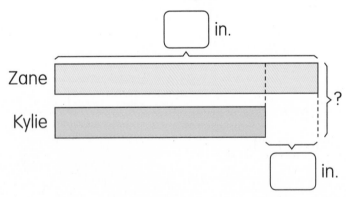

_____ ◯ _____ = _____

Kylie is _____ inches tall.

_____ ◯ _____ = _____

Their total height is _____ inches.

5 A dressmaker has a piece of red cloth 50 inches long.
She cuts 28 inches from the red cloth.
Then, she sews a piece of yellow cloth to the remaining
piece of red cloth.
The piece of yellow cloth is 43 inches long.
What is the length of the cloth now?

How long is the piece of red cloth that is left?

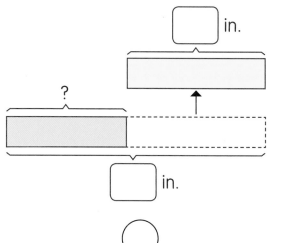

_____ ◯ _____ = _____

The length of red cloth she has left is _____ inches.

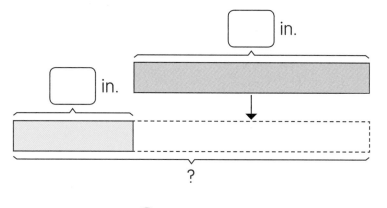

Now, find the new length of the cloth.

_____ ◯ _____ = _____

The length of the cloth now is _____ inches.

6 Ms. Martin has a 600 feet-long rope.
She cuts it into two pieces.
The first piece is 393 feet long.
How much longer is the first piece than the second piece?

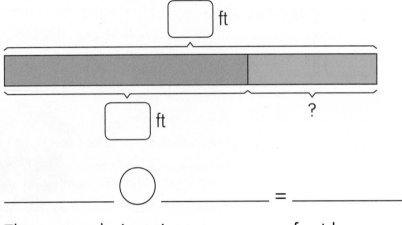

_____ ◯ _____ = _____

The second piece is _____ feet long.

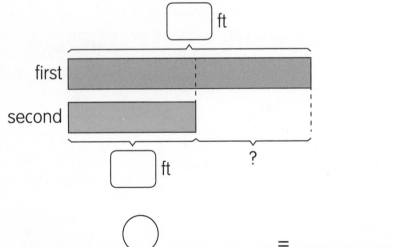

_____ ◯ _____ = _____

The first piece is _____ feet longer than the second piece.

© 2020 Marshall Cavendish Education Pte Ltd

INDEPENDENT PRACTICE

Solve.
Use the bar model to help you.

1 Oliver has two gardens.
His vegetable garden is 240 feet long.
His flower garden is 150 feet long.
How long are both gardens in all?

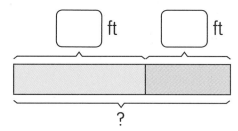

2 Tower A is 705 feet tall.
Tower B is 612 feet tall.
How much taller is Tower A than Tower B?

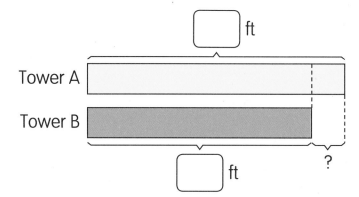

Solve.
Draw a bar model to help you.

3 Stella's rope is 245 inches long.
Ariana's rope is 28 inches longer.
How long is Ariana's rope?

4 Plant A is 60 inches tall.
Plant B is 17 inches shorter.
How tall is Plant B?

5 A wire was cut into three pieces.
The first piece was 34 inches long.
It was 18 inches longer than the second piece.
The second piece was as long as the third piece.

a   How long was the third piece?

b   What was the length of the wire before it was cut?

6 Mr. Young used 500 feet of rope to go around Field A.
He used a rope that was 28 feet shorter for Field B.
How much rope did he use for both fields?

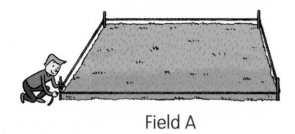

Field A

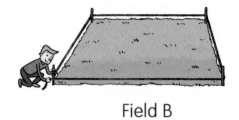

Field B

Mathematical Habit 3 **Construct viable arguments**

Read each statement.
Which statements are incorrect?
Rewrite each incorrect statement to make it correct.

- The classroom door is 6 inches tall.

- The pencil case is 5 feet long.

- The car is 7 feet long.

Problem Solving with Heuristics

① **Mathematical Habit 1** Persevere in solving problems

Jade enters the supermarket.
She wants to go to the meat section.
She must only walk down any path once.

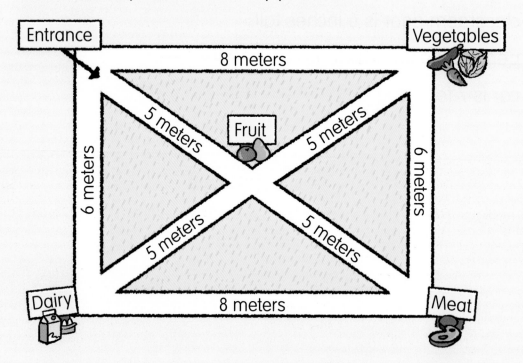

a From the entrance, she walks 14 meters to reach the meat section.
One path she can take is Entrance → Dairy → Meat.
Name the other path she can take if she walks 14 meters to reach the meat section.

b Which is the shortest path from the entrance to the meat section?

c If she walks 22 meters from the entrance to the meat section, which path does she take?

d If she walks 26 meters from the entrance to the meat section, which path does she take?

e Describe another possible path Jade can take from the entrance to reach the meat section.

FRESH MEAT

2 **Mathematical Habit** **1** **Persevere in solving problems**

A rectangular lawn has a length of 50 feet.
A farmer sticks posts along the length of the lawn from Point A to Point B.
If the distance between the posts is 10 feet, how many posts are there?

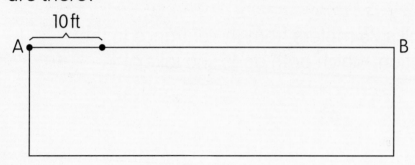

10 ft

A ● ─────── ●   B

? Given three objects, how can you find out which is longer?

Metric Length

Measure

Solve Real-World Problems

Comparing Lengths

The metric units of length are meters (m) and centimeters (cm).

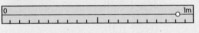

The pair of pants is less than 1 meter long.

The ribbon is 3 centimeters long.

Tree A   Tree B

Tree A is 7 meters tall.
Tree B is 14 meters tall.
Tree B is 7 meters taller than Tree A.
Tree A is 7 meters shorter than Tree B.

Mr. Baker has 17 meters of cloth in his store.
He sells 9 meters of cloth.
How many meters of cloth does he have now?

17 − 9 = 8
He has 8 meters of cloth left.

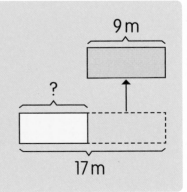

Customary Length

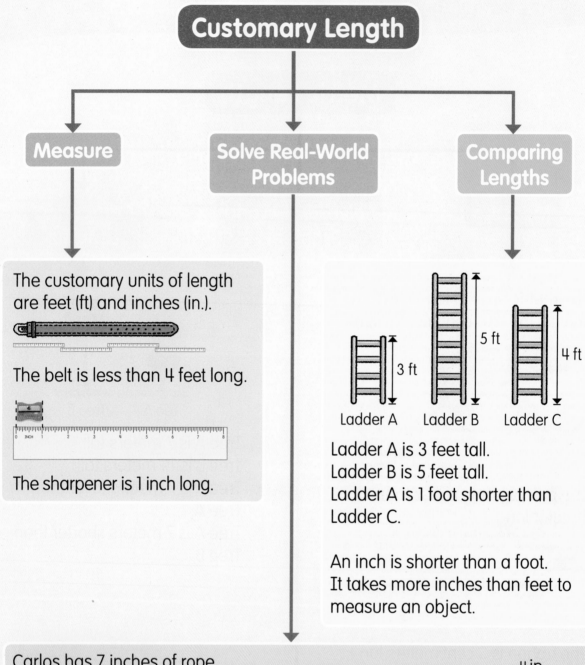

Measure

The customary units of length are feet (ft) and inches (in.).

The belt is less than 4 feet long.

The sharpener is 1 inch long.

Comparing Lengths

Ladder A   Ladder B   Ladder C

Ladder A is 3 feet tall.
Ladder B is 5 feet tall.
Ladder A is 1 foot shorter than Ladder C.

An inch is shorter than a foot. It takes more inches than feet to measure an object.

Solve Real-World Problems

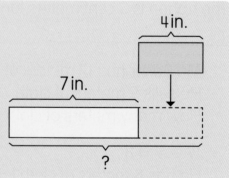

Carlos has 7 inches of rope.
He needs 4 inches more rope to tie a box.
How much rope does he need to tie the box?

$4 + 7 = 11$
He needs 11 inches of rope to tie the box.

Name: _____ Date: _____

Look at each picture.
Fill in each blank.

1

The car is about _____ meters long.

2

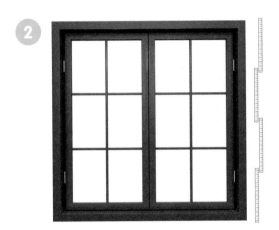

The window is _____ feet tall.

Answer each question.

 Toy dinosaur A is 18 centimeters tall.
Toy dinosaur B is 10 centimeters tall.

Toy dinosaur A

Toy dinosaur B

a   Which toy dinosaur is taller? _____

b   How much taller? _____ centimeters

Measure the length of the ribbon.
Use a centimeter ruler.

The length of the ribbon is _____ centimeters.

Measure the length of the curve.
Use a piece of string and an inch ruler.

5

The length of the curve is _____ inches.

Use a centimeter ruler to draw.

6 Draw a line 5 centimeters long.

7 Draw another line 8 centimeters longer than the above.

Use an inch ruler to draw.

8 Draw a line 5 inches long.

9 Draw a line 2 inches shorter than the above.

Look at the picture.
Answer each question.

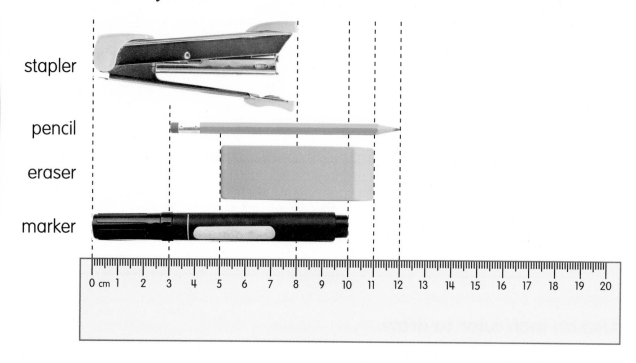

stapler

pencil

eraser

marker

10 What is the length of the marker? _____ centimeters

11 What is the length of the pencil? _____ centimeters

12 Which is longer, the pencil or the marker? _____

13 Which is shorter, the pencil or the eraser? _____

14 How much longer is the stapler than the eraser?
_____ centimeters

15 The longest item is the _____.

16 Order the items from longest to shortest.

_____   _____   _____   _____
    longest   shortest

Write cm or m.

17 The height of a flagpole is about 7 _____.

18 The length of a spoon is about 14 _____.

Write in. or ft.

19 The length of a pencil is about 7 _____.

20 The length of a car is about 15 _____.

Solve.
Draw a bar model to help you.

21 Nicole's book is 21 centimeters long.
Harper's book is 8 centimeters longer.
How long is Harper's book?

Assessment Prep

Answer each question.

22

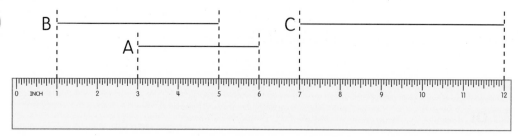

a Which is longer, A or B? _____

b How much longer? _____ in.

c Order the lines from longest to shortest.

_____   _____   _____

    longest   shortest

23 A building is 190 feet tall.
A tree next to it is 150 feet shorter.
Find the total height of the building and the tree.

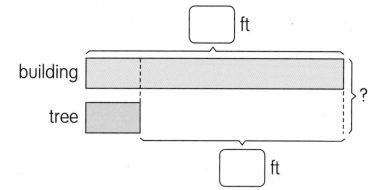

Name: _____   Date: _____

Measurements Around Us

1 The lengths of objects below are either less than 1 meter, more than 1 meter, or about 1 meter.
Write each object in the correct column.

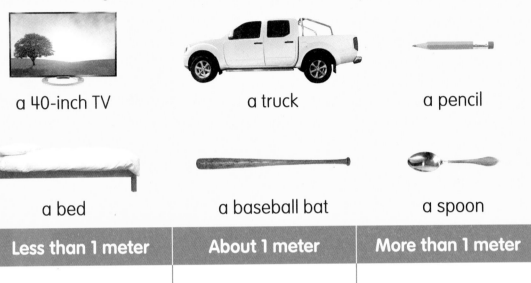

| a 40-inch TV | a truck | a pencil |

| a bed | a baseball bat | a spoon |

Less than 1 meter	About 1 meter	More than 1 meter

2

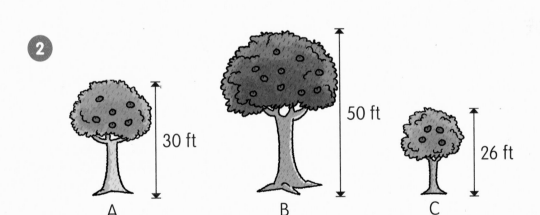

A   30 ft   B   50 ft   C   26 ft

Which tree is the shortest?

How much taller is Tree B than Tree C?

© 2020 Marshall Cavendish Education Pte Ltd

3

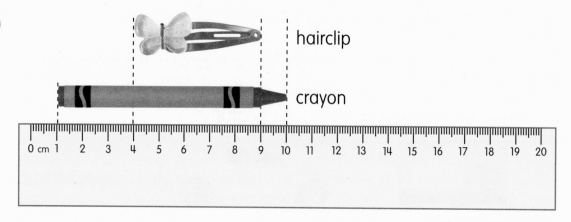

Fill in each blank.

The crayon is _____ centimeters long.

The hair clip is _____ centimeters long.

4

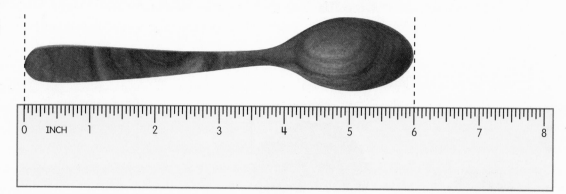

Draw a line that is 2 inches shorter than the spoon.

Rubric

Point(s)	Level	My Performance
7–8	4	• Most of my answers are correct. • I show all my work correctly. • I explain my thinking clearly and completely.
5–6.5	3	• Some of my answers are correct. • I show some of my work correctly. • I explain my thinking clearly.
3–4.5	2	• A few of my answers are correct. • I show little work correctly. • I explain some of my thinking clearly.
0–2.5	1	• A few of my answers are correct. • I show little or no work. • I do not explain my thinking clearly.

Teacher's Comments

STEAM

Class Numbers

How many students are there in your class?
How many classmates ride a school bus?
How many are taller than 4 feet?
How many can jump further than 1 meter?
The answers to these questions are all numbers.
They tell you a lot about your class.

Task

Build a Class Number Wall

Work in pairs or small groups.

1 Make a list of questions you could ask to learn more about your classmates.
Survey your classmates to find answers to your questions.

2 Write your questions and answers on sticky notes. As a class, talk about how to sort them into categories, such as "Taller than 4 feet" or "Jump further than 1 meter."

3 Put the sticky notes on a Class Number Wall. Invite students from other second-grade classes to make Class Number Walls. Compare your numbers.
Discuss what you learned from the results.

Ingredients:

100 grams
of grapes

100 grams
of strawberries

100 grams
of pineapple

150 grams
of yogurt

What do we need to make a fruit salad? What is the total mass of fruit that we need?

Yogurt

Pineapple

Steps:
1. Weigh the correct amount of each ingredient and put them into a mixing bowl.
2. Mix the ingredients well.
3. Place the mixing bowl in the refrigerator for about 4 hours.

How can you find the masses of objects?

Name: _____   Date: _____

Comparing weights

The chick is lighter than the hen.
The hen is heavier than the chick.
The cat is heavier than the hen.
The chick is the lightest.
The cat is the heaviest.

▶ Quick Check

Fill in each blank.

1 pear   cherry

Which is lighter? _____

2 mug   bowl

Which is lighter? _____

3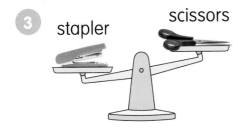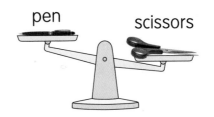

Which object is lighter than the pair of scissors? _____

Which object is heavier than the pair of scissors? _____

Which object is the lightest? _____

4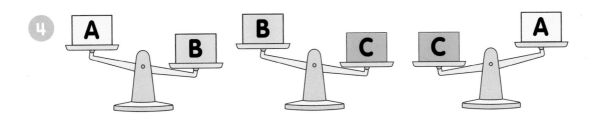

Which box is the heaviest? _____

Measuring weight in units

1 ▨ stands for 1 unit.

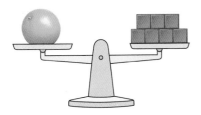

The weight of the orange is about 7 ▨.

The orange is as heavy as 7 units.

▶ **Quick Check**

Look at the picture.
Then, fill in each blank.

Each ⬭ stands for 1 unit.

⑤

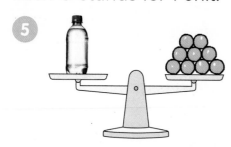

The weight of the bottle of water is about _____ units.

⑥

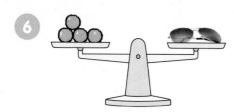

The weight of the sunglasses is about _____ units.

⑦

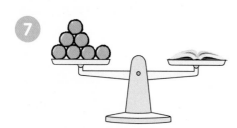

The weight of the book is about _____ units.

Name: _____ Date: _____

Measuring in Kilograms

Learning Objective:
• Measure mass in kilograms.

New Vocabulary
kilogram (kg)
mass
measuring scale

THINK

Which is heavier, the bag of potatoes or the bag of carrots?
How can you tell the mass of each item?

ENGAGE

The large bottle of water and the small bottle of water balance
the box.

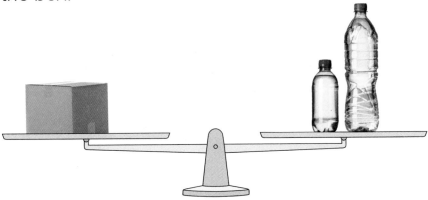

What do you think will happen if:
a   the small bottle is removed?
b   the large bottle is removed?
Which object is heavier? Why do you think so?

1

This is a 1-kilogram mass.

Is it heavier than this bag of flour? Read the measuring scale to find out.

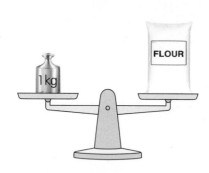

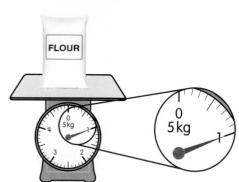

The kilogram is a unit of mass.
kg stands for kilogram.
Read 1 kg as one kilogram.
Kilogram is used to measure the masses of heavier objects.

The bag of flour is as heavy as a mass of 1 kilogram. The mass of the bag of flour is 1 kilogram.

Mass is a measure of how heavy an object is in metric units.

2 What can you say about the mass of the box of tissues?

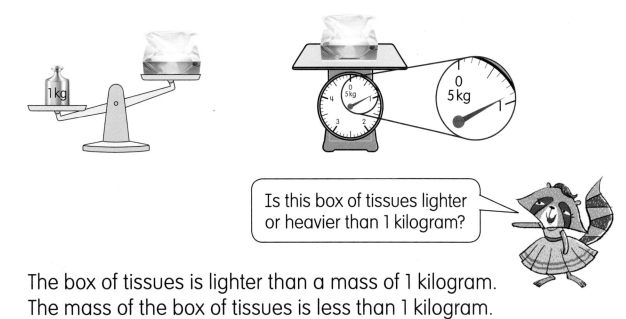

Is this box of tissues lighter or heavier than 1 kilogram?

The box of tissues is lighter than a mass of 1 kilogram.
The mass of the box of tissues is less than 1 kilogram.

3 What can you say about the mass of the carrots?

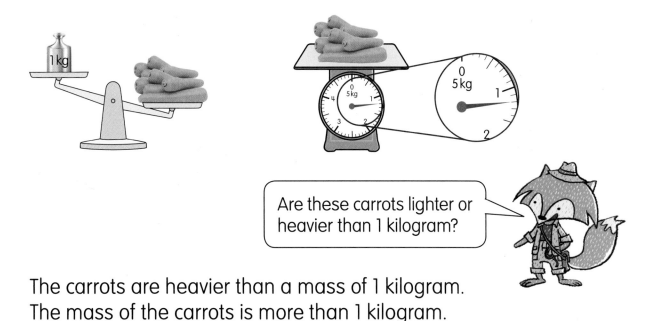

Are these carrots lighter or heavier than 1 kilogram?

The carrots are heavier than a mass of 1 kilogram.
The mass of the carrots is more than 1 kilogram.

Hands-on Activity Using a kilogram to compare masses

(1) Hold a 1-kilogram mass in one hand.

(2) Next, hold a notebook in your other hand.
Which is heavier, the 1-kilogram mass or the notebook?

The _____ is heavier.

(3) Put down the notebook.
Then, pick up your backpack.
Which is heavier, the 1-kilogram mass or the backpack?

The _____ is heavier.

TRY Practice using a kilogram to compare masses

**Compare the mass of each object to the mass of 1 kilogram.
Then, make a ✓ in the correct box.**

1

☐ lighter than 1 kilogram

☐ heavier than 1 kilogram

☐ lighter than 1 kilogram

☐ heavier than 1 kilogram

☐ lighter than 1 kilogram

☐ heavier than 1 kilogram

☐ lighter than 1 kilogram

☐ heavier than 1 kilogram

☐ lighter than 1 kilogram

☐ heavier than 1 kilogram

Brandon removes the 18-kilogram box from this balance scale.

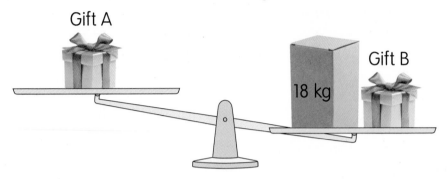

Gift A

Gift B

18 kg

What might happen to the balance scale after Brandon has removed the 18-kilogram box?

LEARN Use scales to find the masses of objects

1 You can use a balance scale to find the masses of objects.

1 kg

The mass of the bag of sugar is 1 kilogram.

Math Talk

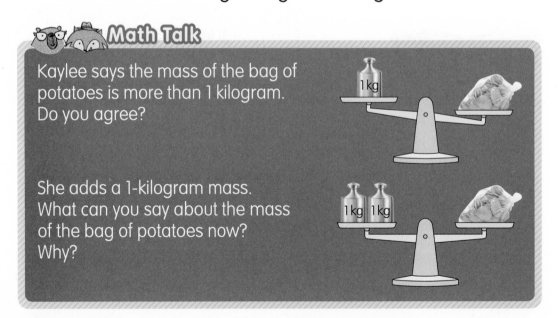

Kaylee says the mass of the bag of potatoes is more than 1 kilogram. Do you agree?

1 kg

She adds a 1-kilogram mass. What can you say about the mass of the bag of potatoes now? Why?

1 kg 1 kg

2 You can also use a kitchen scale to find the masses of objects.

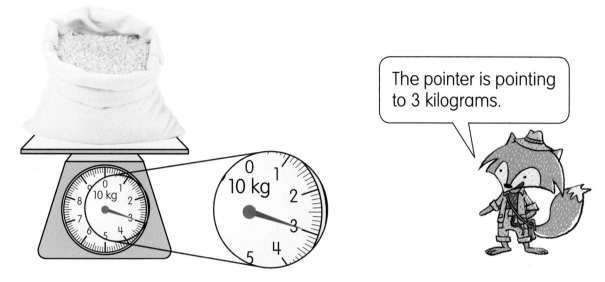

The pointer is pointing to 3 kilograms.

The mass of the bag of rice is 3 kilograms.

TRY Practice using scales to find the masses of objects

Fill in each blank.

1

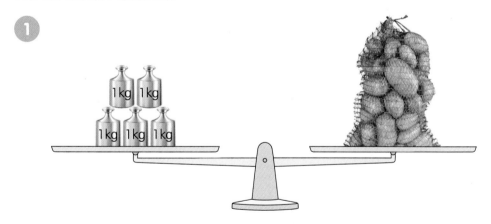

The mass of the bag of potatoes is _____ kilograms.

2

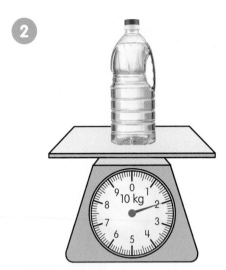

The mass of the bottle of oil is _____ kilograms.

3

The mass of the grapes is _____ kilograms.

ENGAGE

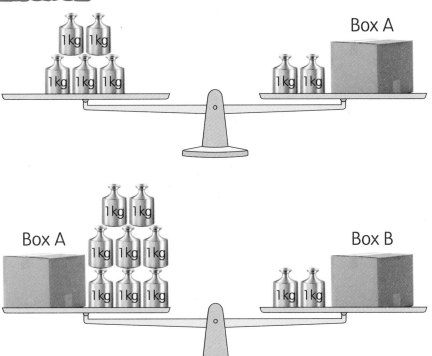

a Find the mass of Box A.

b Find the total mass of Box A and Box B.

LEARN Subtract to find the masses of objects

1 What is the mass of the bag of sand?

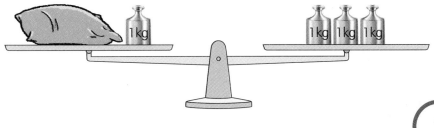

3 − 1 = 2
The mass of the bag of sand is 2 kilograms.

TRY Practice subtracting to find the masses of objects

Subtract to find each mass in kilograms.
Then, fill in each blank.

1

_____ − _____ = _____

The mass of the bag of carrots is _____ kilograms.

2

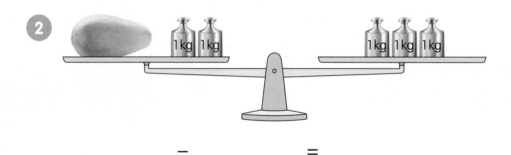

_____ − _____ = _____

The mass of the papaya is _____ kilogram.

3

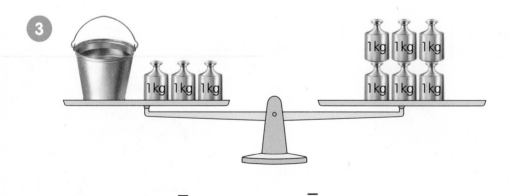

_____ − _____ = _____

The mass of the pail of water is _____ kilograms.

INDEPENDENT PRACTICE

Answer each question.

pineapple

carrots

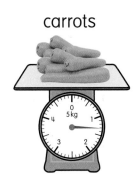

tomato

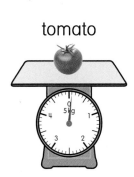

1. Which item has a mass of 1 kilogram? _____

2. Which item is less than 1 kilogram? _____

3. Which item is more than 1 kilogram? _____

Find the mass of each bag of fruit in kilograms.

4.

_____ kg

5.

_____ kg

Subtract to find each mass in kilograms. Then, fill in each blank.

6

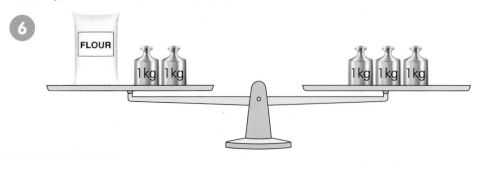

_____ – _____ = _____

The mass of the bag of flour is _____ kilogram.

7

_____ – _____ = _____

The mass of the bag of onions is _____ kilograms.

8

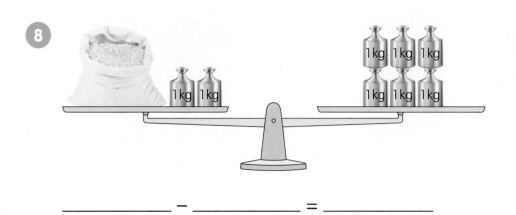

_____ – _____ = _____

The mass of the bag of rice is _____ kilograms.

2 Measuring in Grams

Learning Objective:
• Measure mass in grams.

New Vocabulary
gram (g)

 **THINK**

The total mass of books A, B, and C is shown below.

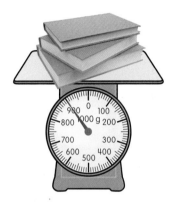

What is the total mass of books A, B, and C?
When Book C is taken away, the scale shows 500 grams.
When books B and C are taken away, the scale shows 200 grams.
What is the mass of Book B?

ENGAGE

Place an eraser on a balance.
Use some 1-gram masses to measure the mass of the eraser.
What is the mass of the eraser?
How do you know?
Now, use a gram scale to check if you are correct.

LEARN Measure masses in grams

1 These are some objects that are lighter than 1 kilogram.

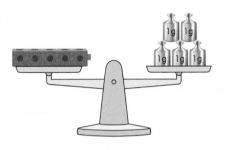

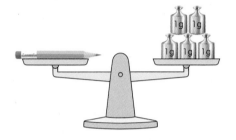

The mass of a cube is about 1 gram.

The mass of the pencil is about 5 grams.

> The gram is a unit of mass.
> g stands for gram.
> Read 1 g as one gram.
> Gram is used to measure the masses of lighter objects.

2 We can use a gram scale to measure the masses of lighter objects.

How do you read the mass?
Look at where the pointer is.
One small marking stands for 10 grams.

450 g

The mass of the lettuce is 450 grams.

TRY Practice measuring masses in grams

Find the mass of each item in grams.

1

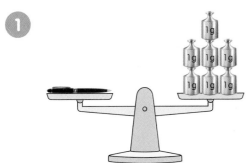

The mass of the pen is _____ grams.

2

The mass of the bunch of bananas is _____ grams.

3

The mass of the gift is _____ grams.

4

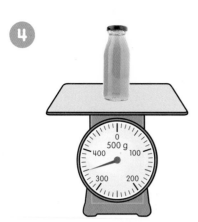

The mass of the bottle is _____ grams.

5

The mass of the grapes is _____ grams.

MATH SHARING

Mathematical Habit 3 Construct viable arguments

Which unit (grams or kilograms) would you use for each object? Why?

1

apple

2

backpack

What is the mass of your backpack?

INDEPENDENT PRACTICE

Find the mass of each item in grams.

1

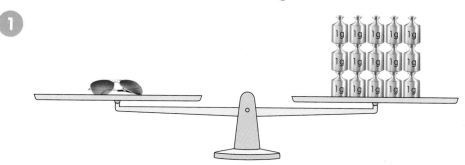

The mass of the sunglasses is _____ grams.

2

The vegetables have a mass of _____ grams.

3

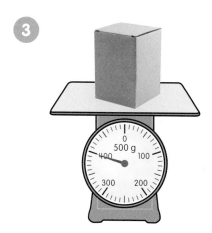

The box has a mass of _____ grams.

Write kg or g in each blank.

4

179 _____

5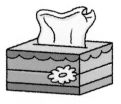

250 _____

6

5 _____

7

300 _____

Decide which scale you would use to find the mass of each item. Then, fill in each blank.

Scale A

Scale B

8 An orange: Scale _____

9 A basket of fruit: Scale _____

10 A computer: Scale _____

11 A watch: Scale _____

3 Comparing Masses in Kilograms and Grams

Learning Objective:
• Compare and order masses in kilograms and grams.

THINK

The total mass of Thomas and Isaac is 150 kilograms.
Thomas's mass is greater than 60 kilograms but less than Isaac's.
What are the possible masses of Thomas and Isaac?

ENGAGE

A fox has a mass of 10 kilograms.
A wolf has a mass of 25 kilograms.
Which is heavier, the fox or the wolf?
If an animal is lighter than the wolf, how can you order the masses of the three animals?
Share your thinking with your partner.

LEARN Compare masses

1
Bag A

Bag B

Bag A has a mass of 3 kilograms.
Bag B has a mass of 2 kilograms.
Bag A is heavier than Bag B.
Bag B is lighter than Bag A.

2

250 g

Sugar

150 g

500 g

The bag of sugar is the lightest object.
The bag of rice is the heaviest object.
From lightest to heaviest, the objects are:

sugar   flour   rice
lightest   heaviest

TRY Practice comparing masses

Look at the pictures.
Then, fill in each blank.

granola bars

cereal

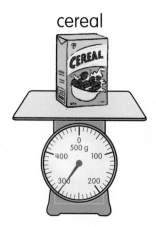

1 What is the mass of the granola bars? _____ grams

2 What is the mass of the cereal? _____ grams

3 The _____ is heavier than the _____.

Look at the pictures.
Write the mass of each object.
Then, answer each question.

④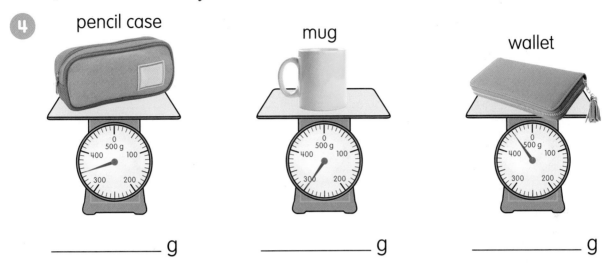

pencil case   mug   wallet

_____ g   _____ g   _____ g

⑤ Which is the lightest? _____

⑥ Which is the heaviest? _____

⑦ Order the objects from lightest to heaviest.

_____   _____   _____

　　lightest   heaviest

⑧ Two of the objects are put on a balance as shown.

What is the other object? _____

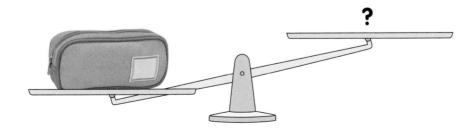

Look at the pictures.
Write the mass of each item.
Then, answer each question.

9

carrots

cabbage

pineapple

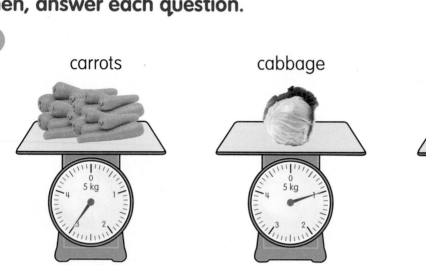

_____ kg   _____ kg   _____ kg

10 Which is the heaviest? _____

11 Which is the lightest? _____

12 Order the items from heaviest to lightest.

_____   _____   _____

   heaviest   lightest

13 Does the picture show what happens when the items are put on a balance? _____

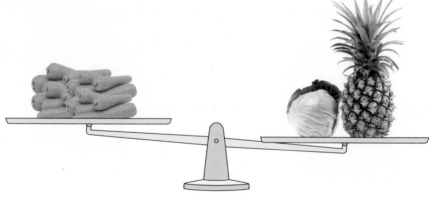

Why?

_____

_____

Name: _____ Date: _____

Look at the pictures.
Then, answer each question.

Bag A    Bag B    Bag C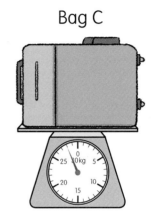

1 The mass of Bag A is _____ kilograms.

2 The mass of Bag B is _____ kilograms.

3 The mass of Bag C is _____ kilograms.

4 Bag A is _____ kilograms heavier than Bag B.

5 Bag B is _____ kilograms lighter than Bag C.

6 The total mass of Bag A and Bag C is _____ kilograms.

7 Order the bags from heaviest to lightest.

_____   _____   _____
   heaviest   lightest

Look at the pictures.
Then, answer each question.

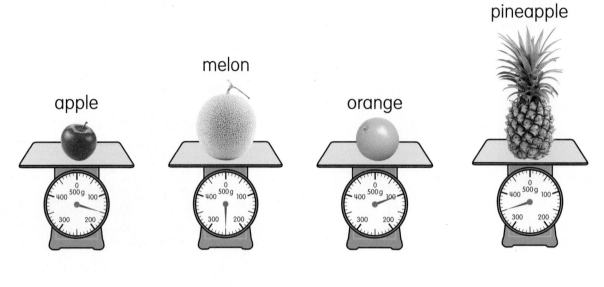

pineapple

melon

apple

orange

8) The mass of the apple is _____ grams.

9) The mass of the melon is _____ grams.

10) The mass of the orange is _____ grams.

11) The mass of the pineapple is _____ grams.

12) The pineapple is _____ grams heavier than the orange.

13) Order the fruit from lightest to heaviest.

_____ _____ _____ _____
    lightest   heaviest

Name: _____   Date: _____

4 Real-World Problems: Addition and Subtraction of Masses

Learning Objective:
• Solve one-step and two-step real-world problems involving mass.

THINK

Grocer A has 16 kilograms of rice.
Grocer B has 9 kilograms of rice.
Grocer B sells double the amount of rice that Grocer A sells.
What is the least amount of rice that Grocer B has left?

ENGAGE

a A bottle of jelly has a mass of 170 grams.
A bottle of tomato ketchup has a mass of 325 grams.

How much heavier is the tomato ketchup than the jelly?
Draw a bar model to show your thinking.

b Michael bought a total of 1 kilogram 655 grams of jelly
and tomato ketchup.
How many bottles of jelly did he buy?

LEARN Solve real-world problems involving addition and subtraction of masses

1. Box A has a mass of 245 grams.
   It is 150 grams lighter than Box B.
   Find the mass of Box B.

   STEP 1 Understand the problem.

   What is the mass of Box A?
   How much heavier is Box B than Box A?
   What do I need to find?

   STEP 2 Think of a plan.
   I can draw a bar model.

   STEP 3 Carry out the plan.

   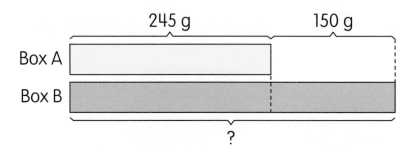

   245 g   150 g

   Box A

   Box B

   ?

   $245 + 150 = 395$

   The mass of Box B is 395 grams.

   STEP 4 Check the answer.
   I can work backwards to check my answer.

   $395 - 150 = 245$
   My answer is correct.

2

I can lift 2 kilograms.

Noah

I can lift 10 kilograms more than Noah!

Zoe

I can only lift 9 kilograms.

Ang

a   What is the mass that Zoe can lift?

b   How much less can Noah lift than Ang?

a

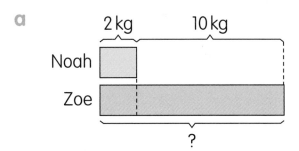

2 kg   10 kg

Noah

Zoe

?

2 + 10 = 12

Zoe can lift 12 kilograms.

b

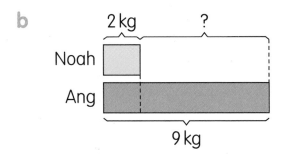

2 kg   ?

Noah

Ang

9 kg

9 – 2 = 7

Noah can lift 7 kilograms less than Ang.

I can work backwards to check my answer.

a   12 – 10 = 2
b   7 + 2 = 9
My answers are correct.

TRY Practice solving real-world problems involving addition and subtraction of masses

Solve.
Use the bar model to help you.

1 A grocer has 78 kilograms of potatoes.
He sells 12 kilograms of potatoes.
How many kilograms of potatoes does he have left?

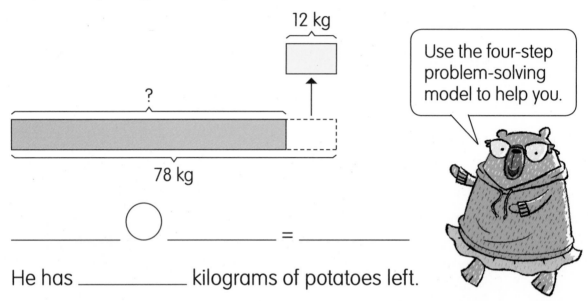

12 kg

?

78 kg

Use the four-step problem-solving model to help you.

_____ ◯ _____ = _____

He has _____ kilograms of potatoes left.

2 The mass of a knight without armor is 61 kilograms.
After putting on the armor, the knight is 49 kilograms heavier.
What is the mass of the knight in armor?

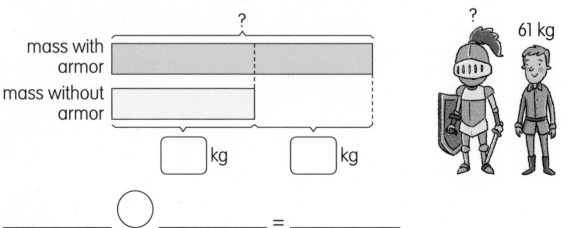

?

mass with armor

mass without armor

?   61 kg

☐ kg   ☐ kg

_____ ◯ _____ = _____

The mass of the knight in armor is _____ kilograms.

3 Ms. Scott has 300 grams of chicken and 250 grams of turkey.
How many grams of meat does she have in all?

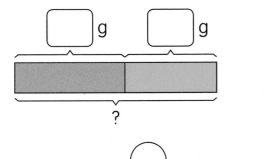

_____ ◯ _____ = _____

She has _____ grams of meat in all.

4 Ms. Miller has 880 grams of pasta.
She uses 320 grams on Monday and 195 grams on Tuesday.
How much pasta does she have left at the end of Tuesday?

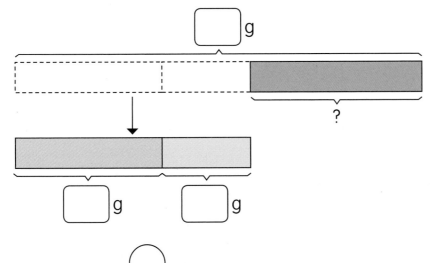

_____ ◯ _____ = _____

She uses _____ grams of pasta on Monday and Tuesday.

_____ ◯ _____ = _____

She has _____ grams of pasta left at the end of Tuesday.

5 Ms. Johnson had 453 grams of nuts.
She ate 134 grams of the nuts.
Then, she bought another 300 grams of nuts.
How many grams of nuts did she have in the end?

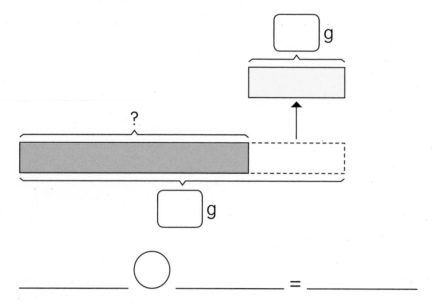

$$\underline{\hspace{2cm}} \bigcirc \underline{\hspace{2cm}} = \underline{\hspace{2cm}}$$

After eating some, she had _____ grams of nuts left.

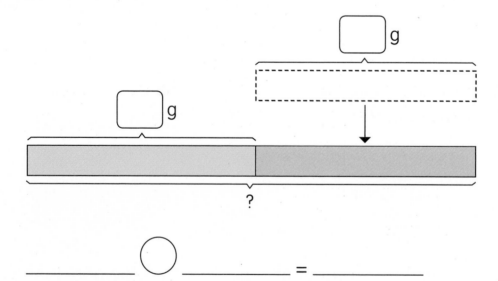

$$\underline{\hspace{2cm}} \bigcirc \underline{\hspace{2cm}} = \underline{\hspace{2cm}}$$

She had _____ grams of nuts in the end.

INDEPENDENT PRACTICE

Solve.
Use the bar model to help you.

1 The mass of a box of cereal is 850 grams.
After the cereal is emptied from the box, the box
is 670 grams lighter.
What is the mass of the empty box?

Use the four-step
problem-solving
model to help you.

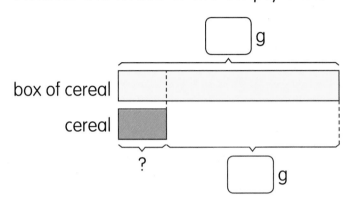

2 A bag of onions has a mass of 240 grams.
A bag of carrots is 230 grams heavier than the bag of onions.
What is the mass of the bag of carrots?

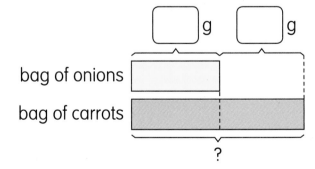

Solve.
Draw a bar model to help you.

3 A farmer has 32 kilograms of corn.
He gives away 16 kilograms of corn to his sister.
He gives away another 10 kilograms of corn to his neighbor.

  a How many kilograms of corn does the farmer give away?

  b How many kilograms of corn does the farmer have left?

4 A factory has 400 kilograms of shrimp.
It bags 120 kilograms on Monday and 100 kilograms on Tuesday.
What is the mass of the shrimp left?

Name: _____ Date: _____

Mathematical Habit 1 **Persevere in solving problems**

Find objects that have a mass of more than 1 kilogram.
Find objects that have a mass of less than 1 kilogram.
Write the objects in the following chart.

1 kg

Lighter	Heavier

Problem Solving with Heuristics

1 **Mathematical Habit 4** **Use mathematical models**

Matthew puts bunches of grapes in a basket and weighs them.
Each bunch of grapes has the same mass.
What is the mass of the basket?

2 | **Mathematical Habit 4** | Use mathematical models

Look at the picture.
Then, answer each question.

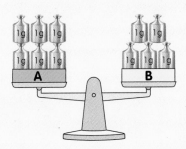

Which is heavier, Box A or Box B?
How much heavier is it?

CHAPTER WRAP-UP

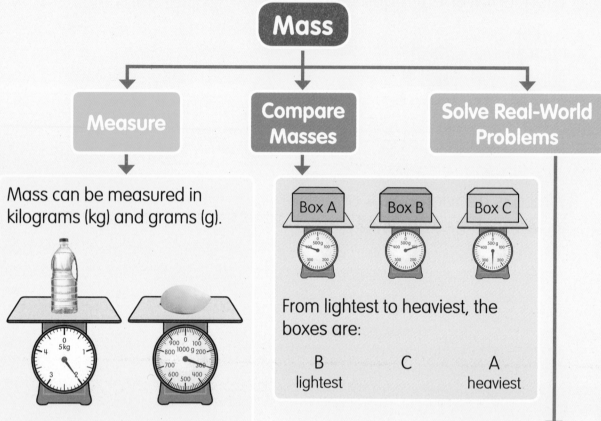

Mass

Measure

Mass can be measured in kilograms (kg) and grams (g).

The mass of the bottle of oil is 2 kilograms.

The mass of the mango is 300 grams.

Add or subtract to find mass.

The mass of the bag is 4 kg.

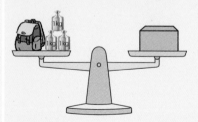

$4 + 3 = 7$
The box has a mass of 7 kilograms.

Compare Masses

Box A   Box B   Box C

From lightest to heaviest, the boxes are:

B   C   A
lightest   heaviest

Solve Real-World Problems

A lemon has a mass of 100 grams. An apple has a mass of 120 grams. What is the total mass of both fruit?

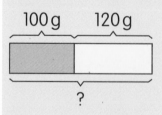

100 g   120 g

?

$100 + 120 = 220$

The total mass of both fruit is 220 grams.

Name: _____ Date: _____

Circle each item that is lighter than 1 kilogram.

1

Look at the pictures.
Write the mass of each item.
Then, fill in each blank.

2 pineapple

bag of rice

papaya

_____ kg _____ kg _____ kg

3 The bag of rice is _____ kilograms heavier than the pineapple.

4 The _____ is the heaviest.

5 Order the items from heaviest to lightest.

_____ _____ _____
heaviest lightest

Look at the pictures.
Write the mass of each item.

6

potatoes

box of cereal

sandwich

_____ g

_____ g

_____ g

7 Order the items from lightest to heaviest.

_____   _____   _____

lightest

heaviest

Write kg or g in each blank.

8   onions

10 _____

9   almonds

300 _____

10   yogurt

125 _____

11   toaster

3 _____

Solve.
Draw a bar model to help you.

12. The total mass of a slice of cheese and a peach is 200 grams.
The mass of the slice of cheese is 28 grams.
What is the mass of the peach?

13. The mass of a chicken is 2 kilograms.
A turkey is 5 kilograms heavier than the chicken.
What is the total mass of the chicken and the turkey?

Assessment Prep

Answer each question.

14 Which of the following shows the mass of the bag of lemons?

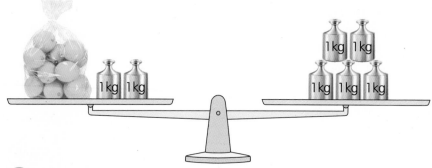

Ⓐ 2 + 3

Ⓑ 3 − 2

Ⓒ 5 − 2

Ⓓ 5 + 2

15 Kimberly has 840 grams of flour.
She uses 210 grams of flour to bake bread.
She gives 250 grams of flour to Jose.
What is the mass of the flour left?

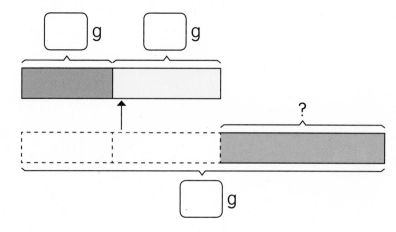

Name: _____ Date: _____

Weighing Ingredients

1 Mr. Lee needs 1 kilogram of apples to bake an apple pie.
He buys some apples.
Are the apples heavier or lighter than 1 kilogram?

Fill in the blank with **heavier** or **lighter**.

The apples are _____ than 1 kilogram.
How do you know?

The mass of the bag of rice is _____ kilograms.

The mass of the turkey is _____ kilograms.

Mr. Lee needs the same mass of rice as the mass of the turkey. How much more rice does he need?

Mr. Lee needs _____ kilogram(s) more rice.

3 Mr. Torres weighs a banana, an orange, and a pineapple. The scales show the mass of the fruit.

Clue 1: The orange is heavier than the banana.
Clue 2: The pineapple is the heaviest.

Draw the correct fruit on each scale.

How much heavier is the pineapple than the banana?

_____

How much lighter is the orange than the pineapple?

_____

Rubric

Point(s)	Level	My Performance
7–8	4	• Most of my answers are correct. • I show all my work correctly. • I explain my thinking clearly and completely.
5–6	3	• Some of my answers are correct. • I show some of my work correctly. • I explain my thinking clearly.
3–4	2	• A few of my answers are correct. • I show little work correctly. • I explain some of my thinking clearly.
0–2	1	• A few of my answers are correct. • I show little or no work. • I do not explain my thinking clearly.

Teacher's Comments

Glossary

A

- **add mentally**

  You can add numbers mentally.
  Find 16 + 3.

  16 + 3 = 19

  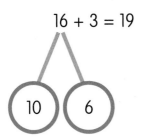

  10   6

B

- **bar model**

  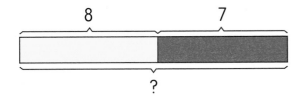

  8   7

  ?

C

- **comparison**

  You draw a comparison model
  to find out which set has more or
  fewer things.

  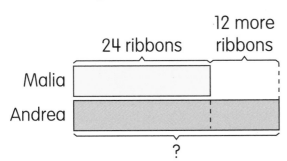

  24 ribbons   12 more ribbons

  Malia

  Andrea

  ?

centimeter (cm)

Centimeter is a metric unit
of length.
Write cm for centimeter.

E

- **expanded form**

  400 + 30 + 2 is the expanded
  form of 432.

F

- **foot (ft)**

  Foot (ft) is a customary
  measurement of length.
  Write ft for foot or feet.

G

- **gram (g)**

  Gram is a metric unit of mass.
  Write g for gram.

  450 g

H

- **hundreds**

  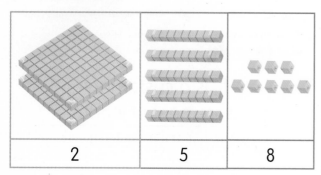

  | 2 | 5 | 8 |

  258 = 2 hundreds 5 tens 8 ones

- **height**

  How tall an object is.

I

- **inch (in.)**

  Inch is a customary
  measurement of length.
  Write inch as in.

  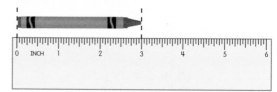

K

- **kilogram (kg)**

  Kilogram is a metric unit
  of mass.
  Write kg for kilogram.

L

- **length**

  How long an object is.

  See **meter**, **centimeter**, **foot**, and **inch**.

M

- ## meter stick

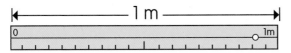

A meter stick is used to measure length.

- ## meter (m)

Meter is a metric unit of length. Write m for meter.

1 m

The car is 3 meters long.

- ## mass

How heavy an object or a set of objects is.

See **kilogram** and **gram**.

- ## measuring scale

This tool measures the mass of an object.

S

- ## standard form

657 is the standard form of 657.

- ## subtract mentally

You can subtract numbers mentally.

Find 18 – 2.

18 – 2 = 16

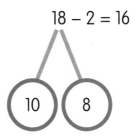

T

- ## thousand

10 hundreds = 1,000

W

- **word form**

  Three hundred twenty-eight is the word form of 328.

- **width**

  How wide an object is.

Index

Pages in **boldface** type show where a term
is introduced.

Manipulative
- 10-sided die, 152
- base 10 blocks, *throughout, see for example,* 7–13, 69–70, 133–134, 156–157, 164–166
- base 10 hundred-square, *throughout, see for example,* 7–13, 32–33, 69–70, 133–134, 164–166
- base 10 rod, *throughout, see for example,* 2–3, 7–13, 69–70, 140, 164–166
- base 10 thousand-cube, 8
- base 10 unit, *throughout, see for example,* 2–3, 32–33, 84, 119–120, 164–166
- connecting cubes, *throughout, see for example,* 183–185, 187–188, 193, 198, 204
- place value strips, 18, 28
- transparent counters, 168, 193

Mass, 360
- comparing, 377–378, 394
    - heavier than, *throughout, see for example,* 356–357, 359–363, 371, 377–378, 391
    - heaviest, 378–382
    - as heavy as, 360
    - lighter than, *throughout, see for example,* 361, 363, 377, 381, 395
    - lightest, 378–382, 394–396
- real-world problems, *see* Real-world problems
- tools
    - balance scale, *see* Balance scale
    - measuring scale, *see* Measuring scale
- units
    - gram (g), *throughout, see for example,* **372**–376, 378–379, 382–384, 394, 396–398
    - kilogram (kg), *throughout, see for example,* **360**–370, 377, 380–381, 394–395, 399–400

Measuring scale, *throughout, see for example,* **360**–361, 365–366, 371, 372, 373–374, 377–380
- pictorial representation, *throughout, see for example,* 360–361, 365–366, 369, 394–396, 400

Mental math
- addition, 52, 64, 108
    - ones to 3-digit number, 80
    - tens and ones, 96
    - tens to 3-digit number, 88
    - within 20, 55–57
    - within 100, 128, 63
- subtraction, 118, 174
    - within 20, 121–123

- within 100, 127
- ones from 3-digit number, 144
- tens from 3-digit number, 151

Meters (m), 260–264, 278–280, 282, 285–286, 340

Meter stick, 259–262, 278
- pictorial representation, *throughout, see for example,* 259–262, 264, 279–280, 286, 345

Numbers
- comparing, *see* Comparisons
- digit, 16
- expanded form, **17**–18, 20–21, 42, 44
- ordering, *throughout, see for example,* 5, 27–28, 30, 42, 45–46
- patterns, 6, 31–35, 39–40, 42, 46–47
- standard form, **17**, 20–21, 42, 44, 47
- word form, **17**–18, 20–21, 42, 44, 47

Number lines
- pictorial representation, 290–292, 295–297, 299, 328, 330

Objects, sets of, 187–196, 204–207

Ones, *throughout, see for example,* 2, 16–22, 91–96, 131–135, 139–142

Operations, *see* Addition; Subtraction

Ordering
- lengths, 277–283, 317–320
- numbers, *throughout, see for example,* 5, 27–28, 30, 42, 45–46

Part-whole model, 187, 246

Patterns, 6, 31–35, 39–40, 42, 46–47

Pictorial representations
- balance scale, *see* Balance scale
- bar models, *see* Bar models
- centimeter ruler, *see* Centimeter ruler
- centimeter tape, *see* Centimeter tape
- foot ruler, *see* Foot ruler
- inch ruler, *see* Inch ruler

measuring scale, *see* Measuring scale
place-value charts, *throughout, see for example,*
   3, 16, 19, 21, 43
meter stick, *see* Meter stick
number lines, *see* Number lines

Place values
   digit, 16, 19–20
   expanded form, **17**–18, 20–21, 42, 44
   hundreds, *throughout, see for example,* **11**,
      68–72, 76, 132–135, 164–166
   ones, *throughout, see for example,* 2, 16–22,
      91–96, 131–135, 139–142
   standard form, **17**, 20–21, 42, 44, 47
   tens, *throughout, see for example,* 2, 68–72,
      76–78, 132–135, 164–166
   word form, **17**–18, 20–21, 42, 44, 47

Place-value charts, *throughout, see for example,* 3,
   16, 19, 21, 43

Place value strips, 18, 28

Real-world problems
   addition, 183–184
      customary lengths, 327–330
      masses, 383–386
      metric lengths, 289–290, 292, 295–296
   one-step, 210, 290, 292
   subtraction, 183–184
      customary lengths, 327–330
      masses, 383–386
      metric lengths, 289–290, 292, 295–296
   two-step, 232–233, 295–296

Sets
   compare, 219–225, 246
   of objects, 187–196, 204–207
   take away, 209, 213, 246

Scale,
   balance, *see* Balance scale
   measuring, *see* Measuring scale

Standard form, **17**, 20–21, 42, 44, 47

Subtraction
   within 20 using mental strategies, 121–123
   within 100

   with regrouping, 126–127
   using mental strategies, 127
   without regrouping, 124–125
within 1,000
   with regrouping, 147–151, 155–160
   without regrouping, 131–135
across zeros, 163–166, 174
metric lengths, 289–296
ones from 3-digit number mentally, 144
with regrouping, *throughout, see for example,*
   120, 126–127, 139–142, 147–150, 155–169
without regrouping, 119, 124–125, 131–135,
   174, 182
real-world problems, *see* Real-world problems
tens from 3-digit number mentally, 151

Taking away, 203, 209, 213, 246

Tens, *see* Place values

Thousand, **8**

Tools (of measure), *see* Length; Mass

Transparent counters, 168, 193

Units (of measure), *See* Length; Mass

Units of length
   centimeters (cm), *throughout, see for example,*
      266–276, 281–284, 287–289, 346–349, 352
   foot (ft), *throughout, see for example,* **304**–308,
      318, 320, 322–328, 344–345
   inches (in.), **309**–314, 318–321, 322–324
   meters, **260**–264, 278–280, 282, 285–286, 340

Width, **260**–261, 266, 269, 305, 307

Word form, **17**–18, 20–21, 42, 44, 47

Zero
   subtracting across, 163–166, 174

Photo Credits

Chakrapong Worathat/123rf.com, ii) © Goce Risteski/123rf.com, iii) © Alekss/Dreamstime.com, 351(ml to mr): i) © Happy Stock Photo/Shutter Stock, ii) © Gino Santa Maria/123rf.com, iii) © Igor Kovalchuk/123rf.com, 352(t to b): i) © sunstock/iStock, ii) © Charles Brutlag/123rf.com, iii) © Tippawan Thanatornwong/123rf.com, 354tr: © Andy Nowack/iStock, 354mr: © Yuganov Konstantin/Shutter Stock, 355: © Weedezign/iStock, 355b: © HAKINMHAN/iStock, 356ml: © Viktor Prymachenk/Dreamstime.com, 356mm: © utima/123rf.com, 356bl: © Svyatoslav Lypynskyy/123rf.com, 356bm: © Sommai Larkjit/123rf.com, 357(tl to tr): i) © Sarawutnam/iStock, ii) © Ольга Еремина/123rf.com, iii) © Prapan Ngawkeaw/123rf.com, iv) © Ольга Еремина/123rf.com, 357bl: © Phive2015/Dreamstime.com, 358(t to b): i) kornienko/123rf.com, ii) visivasnc/123rf.com, iii) © Mike Flippo/123rf.com, 359tm: © Andrey Eremin/123rf.com, 359tm: © Diana Taliun/123rf.com, 359(bl to br): i) © Africa Studio/ Shutter Stock, ii) © kornienko/123rf.com, iii) © kornienko/123rf.com, 360m: © Alexander Kharchenko/123rf.com, 361t: © Sommai Damrongpanich/123rf.com, 361m: © Lotus Images/Shutter Stock, 363(tl to bl): i) © Vitaly Zorkin/Shutter Stock, ii) © Veniamin Kraskov/Dreamstime.com, iii) © Polryaz/123rf.com, iv) © Irina Belokrylova/123rf.com, v) © Veeranat Suwangulrut/123rf.com, 364(tl to tr): i) © Timmary/123rf.com, ii) © Dimitrii Kazitsyn/Shutter Stock, iii) © Timmary/123rf.com, 364m: © Oleksii Terpugov/123rf.com, 364br: © kariphoto/123rf.com, 365tl: © serezniy/123rf.com, 365m: © Nataliia Pyzhova/123rf.com, 366tl: © Alexandr Kornienko/Dreamstime.com, 366ml: © Aedka Studio/Shutter Stock, 367ml: © Africa Studio/Shutter Stock, 368(t to b): i) © Diana Taliun/123rf.com, ii) © Satit Srihin/123rf.com, iii) © Akinshin/Dreamstime.com, 369(tl to tr): i) © oleksiy/123rf.com, ii) © Lotus Images/Shutter Stock, iii) © MCE, 369(bl to br): i) © Lindavostrovska/Dreamstime.com, ii) © Lunx (null)/Dreamstime.com, 370(t to b): i) © Alexander Kharchenko/123rf.com, ii) © hawk111/iStock, iii) © serezniy /123rf.com, 371tl: © Brian Jackson/123rf.com, 372(tl to tr): i) © MCE. Objects sponsored by Noble International Pte Ltd., ii) © Alekss/Dreamstime.com, 372bl: © Alfio Scisetti/123rf.com, 373(t to b): i) © Prapan Ngawkeaw/123rf.com, ii) © Natee Trireaklith/123rf.com, iii) © Timmary/123rf.com, 374tl: © siraphol/123rf.com, 374ml: © yurakp/123rf.com, 374bl: © utima/123rf.com, 374bm: © Kadrof/Dreamstime.com, 375(t to b): i) © visivasnc/123rf.com, ii) © Mohammed Anwarul Kabir Choudhury/123rf.com, iii) © Dmitrii Kazitsyn/Shutter Stock, 377bl: © Dmitry lerashov/123rf.com, 377bm: © Kadrof/Dreamstime.com, 379(tl to tr): i) © goh seok thuan/Shutter Stock, ii) © levgenii Meyer/

Shutter Stock, iii) © Pongsak Tawansaeng/123rf.com, 379bl: © goh seok thuan/Shutter Stock, 380(tl to tr): i) © Lotus Images/Shutter Stock, ii) © JIANG HONGYAN/Shutter Stock, iii) © MCE, 380(bl to br): i) © Lotus Images/Shutter Stock, ii) © JIANG HONGYAN/Shutter Stock, iii) © MCE, 382(tl to tr): i) © utima/123rf.com, ii) © Acha Yhamruksa/123rf.com, iii) © Phive2015/Dreamstime.com, iv) © MCE, 383bm: © siraphol/123rf.com, 383bm: © Natalya Aksenova/123rf.com, 391: Created by Fwstudio - Freepik.com, 392tl: © Sergey Kolesnikov/123rf.com, 392tm: © Sergey Kolesnikov/123rf.com, 394ml: © Alexandr Kornienko/Dreamstime.com, 394ml: © Ekaterina_Simonova/iStock, 395(tl to tr): i) © SergeBertasiusPhotography/Shutter Stock, ii) © Eric Isselee/123rf.com, iii) © Hayati Kayhan/123rf.com, iv) © Houghton Mifflin Harcourt, 395(ml to mr): i) © MCE, ii) © serezniy/123rf.com, iii) © Satit Srihin/123rf.com, 396ml: © MrVitkin/Dreamstime.com, 396mr: © Alexey Yuminov/123rf.com, 396bl: © Marazem/Dreamstime.com, 396br: © Svetlana Voronina/123rf.com, 398tl: © Lindavostrovska/Dreamstime.com, 399tl: © Ivonne Wierink/123rf.com, 400tl: © serezniy/123rf.com, 400tr: © ishtygashev/123rf.com, 403tr: © Charles Brutlag/123rf.com, 404tl: © Alfio Scisetti/123rf.com, 404tr: © Charles Brutlag/123rf.com, 404mr: © Dmitry lerashov/123rf.com, 405ml: © Maksim Toome/123rf.com

NOTES

NOTES

NOTES

© 2020 Marshall Cavendish Education Pte Ltd

Published by Marshall Cavendish Education
Times Centre, 1 New Industrial Road, Singapore 536196
Customer Service Hotline: (65) 6213 9688
US Office Tel: (1-914) 332 8888 | Fax: (1-914) 332 8882
E-mail: cs@mceducation.com
Website: www.mceducation.com

Distributed by
Houghton Mifflin Harcourt
125 High Street
Boston, MA 02110
Tel: 617-351-5000
Website: www.hmhco.com/programs/math-in-focus

First published 2020

ISBN 978-0-358-10179-6

Printed in Singapore

1 2 3 4 5 6 7 8   1401   25 24 23 22 21 20
4500759314   A B C D E

The cover image shows a Pygmy slow loris.
These animals can be found in Southeast Asia.
They live in forests and feed on insects, tree parts, and fruit.
A Pygmy slow loris has a round head, narrowed nose and big forward-facing eyes.
It only comes out at night.
Its big eyes help it to find food in the dark.